Live Life Like A Bumble Bee:

Everyday Opportunities To Grow and Develop

Anthony Lyle Smith

Live Life Like A Bumble Bee:

Everyday Opportunities To Grow and Develop

Dedication

This book is dedicated to everyone who I know and everyone that I am yet to know – I am looking forward to learning from you. Thank you for the loving support and encouragement Honey!

Thank you for being there when I needed you,
Thank you for being there when I didn't need you,

Thank you for caring when I needed you too
Thank you for caring when I didn't need you too

Thank you for sharing with me
Thank you for allowing me to share with you

Thank you for the opportunity to learn with you
Thank you for the opportunity to learn from you

Thank you for trusting in me
Thank you for letting me trust in you

Thank you for loving me
Thank you for letting me love you

Thank you for letting me be me
Thank you for you being you

Thank you for the good times
Thank you for the bad times

Thank you for being family when you were
Thank you for being family when you weren't

About The Author

"Don't walk the well trodden path of others,
Rather walk creating your own path where others may choose to follow"
A.L.S.

Anthony was born and raised in South Africa, in a multi-racial, multi-lingual upbringing. From an early age, the local Zulu's named him Khaghla (pronounced kesh-la), which is the Zulu name, meaning "old man," or "wise man" or "mature man." He was given the name by the Zulu Natives because of his nature - like a "wise old man" who seemed to know when something has happened or is going to happen, not being fooled by anyone – mature for his age.

Today, after many years of extensive traveling and working around the world, Anthony can be found in Ireland where he is a well qualified Holistic Health Therapist, and Proprietor of *The Little House of Avalon Ltd.* (See the web at (http://www.littlehouseofavalon.com) A Holistic Health Farm and Related Education Center in the County of Roscommon, Ireland.

Prior to settling in Ireland with his wife Bernadette, he worked together with her in Germany and in South Africa, whilst continuing his studies.

Currently managing the Health Center and assisting clients on their Pathway's of Choice, he also teaches a varied form of Foot Reflexology, "Holistic Light Art Foot Reflexology" That is rapidly becoming a sought after Therapy.

Anthony has also developed a safe and manipulation-free form of self-help for Back and Body, called "Back-Smith" - part of his Body Management Solution ® Program, which is in the pipeline for books, along with various other forms of Therapy.

Anthony's mother developed Arthritis when he was about eight years old, and from this time he has been working with people in pain, discomforts and the issues that are associated with these ailments.

It was here that his adventurous "journey" began, and to this day continues to work for the well being of individual Holistic Health (body, mind and soul).

Khaghla resides in Taughmaconnell, Ireland with his; partner, spiritual-advisor, Co-worker and best wife a man could ask for, and their many children - two and four legged, (some feathered), which have been neglected or thrown out from some place or another.

They have also established an Association for Therapists and Alternative Approach Health Practitioners, who are very gentle in their work, called *"The Web of Light,"* which is a link to Alternative practitioners from around the globe. For more information you can go to the web: http://www.weboflight.org

For more information, questions or comments feel free to send e-mail to: littlehouseofavalon@eircom.net

Alternatively feel free to write to:

Anthony Lyle Smith
The Little House of Avalon
Ballyreevagh
Taughmaconnell
Ballinasloe
County Roscommon
Ireland

Tel. /Fax 00 353 905 83002

How To Use This Information

The first read should be a cover to cover, and thereafter you can refer to those chapters that you need a refresher on.

It is a lot easier to find solutions when you are provided with the right information, so choose for yourself the information that you need.

Many of the chapters will have information that may be used in other areas of life too, so enjoy a good read and apply the information where it suits YOU best.

TABLE OF CONTENTS

PREFACE.. 15
INTRODUCTION... 19
CHAPTER 1 SELF-EMPOWERMENT 23
CHAPTER 2 HEALTH BASICS 29
CHAPTER 3 MATERIAL ASSETS OR INVALUABLE
POSSESSIONS?.. 34
CHAPTER 4 FRUSTRATION MEETS LOVE 38
CHAPTER 5 ADVICE OR ADVISE 42
CHAPTER 6 BELIEFS 45
CHAPTER 7 RELATIONSHIPS OF UNDERSTANDING .. 47
CHAPTER 8 ASSUMPTION 49
CHAPTER 9 INTUITION 54
CHAPTER 10 THE WHEEL OF LIFE.................................... 56
CHAPTER 11 I AM LISTENING AND I HEAR YOU........... 65
CHAPTER 12 THE CLOSER, THE HARDER? 68
CHAPTER 13 ARE YOU REALLY GUILTY? 72
CHAPTER 14 BE OPEN, HONEST & DISREGARD THE
REST 74
CHAPTER 15 THE PIT OF UNDERSTANDING 78
CHAPTER 16 STRESS 83
CHAPTER 17 NAKED PEOPLE ALL WANT THE SAME
THING!.. 87
CHAPTER 18 A MISTAKE OR A LESSON OPPORTUNITY
.... 90
CHAPTER 19 ATTACK OR WITHDRAW.......................... 94
CHAPTER 20 WHO IS PRESSING YOUR BUTTONS &
WHY?.. 97
CHAPTER 21 I WOULD IF..., I SHOULD...BUT... 100
CHAPTER 22 THE BUMBLE BEE 102
CHAPTER 23 PROCESS 104
CHAPTER 24 A ROSE AMONGST THE THORNS 106

CHAPTER 25 LEADING BY EXPERIENCE...................... 108
CHAPTER 26 EXPECTATION.. 111
CHAPTER 27 THE FISHERMAN & THE WEALTHY
BUSINESSMAN.. 113
CHAPTER 28 MORE IS NOT ALWAYS BETTER? 115
CHAPTER 29 DIET 118
CHAPTER 30 THE NOT EATING PROPERLY, OR TOO
LITTLE DIET... 126
CHAPTER 31 CULTURE AND TRADITION VS Y2K 132
CHAPTER 32 BOUNDARY'S & LIMITS............................ 135
CHAPTER 33 MISTAKES OR LESSONS............................ 139
CHAPTER 34 CHOICE.. 142
CHAPTER 35 GOALS & ACCOMPLISHMENTS.............. 150
CHAPTER 36 YOUR GIFT TO THE WORLD.................... 155
CHAPTER 37 LAST WORDS 158

Preface

The Bumble Bee is a humble creature,
It goes about doing its own thing not bothering anyone
It weighs only two grams, and has a wing surface area of 2cm squared
According to the laws of physics, and aviation
With these dimensions it should be impossible to fly
But - the bumblebee knows of no such limits
And continues to fly doing it's own things.

This is the opportunity that lies ahead of you - to Live Life Like a Bumblebee.

By being you, it ensures a good quality life, filled with the joys and trials of learning how to live most successfully. It also ensures a fair exchange of information, which enables you to learn as you move forward in life. My late mother taught me this, and it is very true - which means that by you reading this I have something to exchange with you, and you in turn have something to exchange with me.

"Be yourself no matter where you are or whatever you are doing, because the only people that will ever be around you, are those people who will benefit from you and visa-versa."

On a daily basis, I get new clients - clients that have been everywhere and not been able to find understanding of their difficulties, and often after just one consultation they have a complete new awareness of themselves and how they are (not) living THEIR life, but the life "friends," colleagues and relatives prefer them to live.

We all have our problems and our own way to deal with them. Every now and again however, you may find something or someone that makes dealing with certain difficulties easier than your particular way. It may have been something that you overheard, a radio personality, interview on T.V., words from the script of a film, or as in this case, a book you happened to come across.

This book is just that. It's the information to make life that much easier. The information contained within the pages of these books has already helped thousands of people around the world, now you have been drawn to it - try it!

Another persons' perspective is sometimes all it takes. We live our lives the way we have always lived - and in this manner we will continue to live, until it no longer works anymore. Most of my days are spent talking to clients about their difficult areas and things going on in their lives.

Often it is enough for a client to simply speak their mind, and feel heard - and then other times, people find it difficult to understand their own thoughts /life-patterns and what is going on within their life which is where they need guidance.

The object of this book is for me to share my views on areas of daily life that we all face at one time or another along the way. Many clients have benefited from being able to "see" their life from my perspective, which allows them to view their own life, as other people would see them.

Each of their problems and personal complaints have completely different backgrounds, (as we are all our own individuals) from a different upbringing however, the areas of their lives in which they are "stuck," and the view being taken in many of the cases is common, "What will people say or think If I DO NOT Do what they ask of me?"

With this being the case, I feel it a privilege being asked by these individuals, to help them help "themselves," to deal with their own issues in the way that best compliments their personality, lifestyle and immediate circumstances. This means that they have to make their own decisions as to who they are in this make-up. When choices need to be made, I provide them with an informative way of making those choices as "easy" to make as possible.

The object of this book is to make this information available to many more people who may not realize how complicated people have allowed our lives to become, and the "tools" with which this complexity can be simplified. There are many topics in different areas of life, and daily examples to make the concepts easier to understand.

Dealing with so many different cases during the years, I have come to realize where the greatest area's of guidance is needed, and it is this information, which I have compiled an easy to understand level with plenty of examples.

I wish you a wonderful, exiting and adventurous journey.

Introduction

The Art Of Bumble Bee Flying

"By becoming aware of your true consciousness - you are able to act on true thoughts, feelings, emotions and ideals rather than those influenced by family, society and others within your environment "

"In order to know where you are going, you have got to know where you have been"

- Are you dissatisfied with your life in any way?
- Is there too much that seems to always be just out of
  reach, leaving you unfulfilled and frustrated?
- Do you feel caught in a vicious circle of non-accomplishment?
- Do you wish there was an easier approach to daily
  life?

If "YES", then by reading this, you have taken a good step in the right direction.

In today's modern society, many people measure their accomplishments and achievements by material success. These people feel that they have failed if they are not driving an expensive car bigger and better than their neighbors, live a top lifestyle, and of course have the house with expensive fittings to boot.

But, surely there is more to life than what your neighbors or anyone else does or does not have. Should it not be about accumulating invaluable assets of nonmaterial value, which can be used daily and don't depreciate

19

with time; rather, become more valuable. The most priceless assets I am referring to - are those of ones personal consciousness and individuality.

Through the processes and the "work" in this book, you will begin to generate a clearer understanding of the concepts - your consciousness will become your greatest asset filling you with personal satisfaction that no material possession will ever offer you.

Become aware of your true consciousness! This will enable you to act on true thoughts, feelings, emotions and ideals rather than those of your family, society and others found within your environment.

It sounds good, but be aware that the words you will read will not make it better overnight. Success comes through dedicated hard work, and commitment to you. It is this formula which will assist you in becoming the REAL you.

The information being offered to you is through my personal life experiences. Experiences of another individual may never come close to where you may be in your own life journey, but may provide you with insight into other approaches of living life. How you choose to use the information is entirely up to you. But what is important is that you "TAKE RESPONSIBILITY FOR YOUR OWN ACTIONS"

I have experienced the turmoil that life can become on a day-to-day basis, with emotional disturbance caused by thoughts of frustration, and what feels like there is no end in sight.

At one stage, I felt really stuck with no foreseeable outcome, a way out seemed impossible, and a positive outcome - as likely me being the next man to walk on the moon.

The experiences themselves are perhaps very different from yours, but through mine, you may recognize your own thought patterns and emotional responses to certain situations. Through this I offer you the information and tools, which guided me out of many situations, enabling me to grow from strength to strength into a proud and fulfilled individual that I am today.

Only a few years down the road, I can say that I have also achieved some of the major goals I set for myself in less time that I planned, and they continue to grow by the day into new ones.

Within a short space of time, (and I don't mean years), you too can quickly grow and begin to achieve your own goals. Like a plant, if you nurture it, it will thrive and do very well quickly, however an unnourished plant will die off within a few days.

"A journey of a thousand miles begins with the first step"
Confucius, Philosopher

Chapter 1

Self-Empowerment

"I allow myself to be myself"

We all have to start this journey somewhere so, regardless of your issue, be it: money, health, or happiness you need to ask yourself one thing: " Do I love myself and am I willing to change?" YES?
Then say to yourself out loud " I do love myself and I am willing to change!"

If you love yourself, nothing will stand in your way, not even saying this out aloud and having people in the same room look at you sideways. If you love yourself, you are number 1 in your life - others come after you, even your family, and this can be done without feeling guilty. Through the acceptance of yourself and of who you really are, you will feel free to change when you feel ready to without negativity around the thoughts of what others may think.

You can do this for yourself by putting yourself first, then you are doing the best thing for your family and friends, because if you are not happy with yourself, you are going to be negative inside and this will radiate out ultimately affect the situation within your environment, so do it for yourself, and indirectly for them. When you can feel good for being yourself, then others will feel good for you.

Free yourself of your past by letting go. Your past has created the person you are today. Everything has happened for a reason; even the really unpleasant thing in life. Look for the lesson being offered not to the memory of an unpleasant experience.

Nature will always provide a balance - it's up to you to find it, and that is how the growth and learning occurs.

Many people have commented at the beginning of sessions about not wanting to burden me with their problems, "What would you know about problems anyway - look at you!"

I understand now after many years, that people have put me up on a pedestal, but for a long time I did not realize that people saw me in that light.

When people do that "praising" of another individual who they look up to and respect - they somehow seem to see you as being "perfect" (said tongue in cheek) without a problem, or never had a problem

From the time I realized this, I began the habit of telling people that if I am not feeling 100%, then that's how I am feeling - and when I am having a really bad day then that is what I share with them.

This is simply to show them that I am not from a planet that creates "perfect people", but am just as prone to good days and bad as they are although by looking after myself health-wise, I tend to have more good days than bad.

Take the lesson opportunity and the lesson provided is to be remembered. With that experience behind you and the lesson learned at hand, you can move forward as a stronger individual that before the lesson.

If you are not sure what the lesson was, then look at what is going on within your life. Take a piece of paper and write down your situation before the event and then ask yourself what information is being provided by the event (good and not good) to help resolve your situation ...be true to yourself.

But, to answer those people who have on many occasion asked what I might know of negative experiences - I tell them the same as I tell all the others - MY LESSON.

I could tell them that my mother developed a crippling disease when I was already young - (about 8 years old) and my father is an alcoholic (now recovered – about 14 years clean). I could also tell them that from what I remember, my childhood was not as entertaining as most of my friends - not being able to have many friends, because it would mean bringing them round to see my crippled mom, and then on weekends - my usually drunk and embarrassing father.

I did not have as much time for the first 6-7 years after that because I somehow being youngest seemed to be nominated to stay home and "mom-sit", maybe it was not that way - but it's how I remember it. Then when someone else was about the house - like a shot I would be gone.

I could also tell people that when you are young at school and all is "normal" at home, at birthdays you would have a party and all your friends would come over, even sleep over, go out for a burger or to the games arcade - I had one!

I did only have one birthday sleep over, which finally woke me up. I finally had the courage to have about 5 friends around for a birthday, and dad came home drunk.

And it began - the lads abused my dad something senseless - from farting powder in his tea and sprinkled on his dinner, to feeding him laxative chocolate to teasing him and making a fool out of him because he was so drunk - I woke up!!

These were a bunch of 12 year olds making a complete arse of my dad, which would be spoken about for months to come at school. I did not have any more secrets about home after that night and now that I look back at it - it was a blessing in disguise. The lads were entertained and I did not have to be secretive about home anymore.

Shortly after this, we honestly told dad how we felt about his alcohol abuse, and he agreed o go into a treatment center for a number of weeks - and we have not looked back since CONGRATULATIONS DAD!!

Mom in the meanwhile became worse and worse and my time seemed to become less and less for the lads and me. In mom's last 2 ½ years we managed to get her a Nurse Aid- Faith Dube, what a lovely woman.

This was so that we could more or less get on with our lives and gets focused on our educations. Which never happened, mom and I were too close and I worried about her all the time?

Then it got to the stage in life, hers and ours where we wanted her to pass on because she was always in such pain, always threatening to overdose because she felt such a burden on the rest of us and it at that point in time would have been best. Surgery was out for joint replacement because she had become too weak and would not have survived surgery. 12 June 1993 she was suddenly dead.

My middle sister came and told me that morning - knocked on my door, "moms dead", she said, "don't talk crap" was my response before seeing the tears in her eyes.

Suddenly it was real, after going on for about 10 years – "THE END"- like in the films. My eldest sister and Faith the nurse, administered CPR until the ambulance arrived, and then the paramedics crew declared her dead after doing their own bit - that was when I was woken.

I remember the image on her face when I saw her for the last time that morning - such peace, and a sense of rest on her face for the first time in I don't know how long.

The day of course was an emotional one, filled with celebration and sadness. We were all very sad and felt shocked - when someone's gone, they are gone and that's it - there is no coming back! And that reality hit hard, but after the funeral we were all able to get a start on our lives.

So what life experience do I have that could be learned from?

All this kind of thing going on for years was at the time not great or exciting for me at all. But this is what I did get from it:

1. Nearly every afternoon after school for all those tears, mom and I would sit and chat while I ate lunch. I got to know her better than I possibly ever would have, because she found it easy to talk to me, and I learned to listen.

2. Learning to listen taught me great patience, and is today one of my greatest assets.

3. I learned a great deal about pain and discomfort, from the horse mouth, and from on-hand interactive experience, which no textbook could ever come close to.

4. It was a young age at which I started getting involved with interacting on a "healing" level, always able to find and massage that sore spot, or to ease that pain, which others could not, sometimes not even the drugs - which became an addiction.

5. I learned about people with addictions and what it is like to live with them, but also how they work and how the rehabilitation system works - my father with alcohol and my mother with her Drugs that were called medication.

6. I learned what it is like to go without the niceties that many of my friends had, this taught me the value of money.

7. I learned to interact within the adult realm of thought and communication too.

8. I learned valuable lessons as to what is acceptable and what is not to me.

9. I learned about individuality... And that people are different from one another.

10. I learned that life is not the same through everyone's eyes.

There are many lessons that I learned and will continue to learn from them as become aware of them.

So to be yourself is very important, and to take from your own life's opportunities those lessons being provided. You shall only grow, if that is the least that happens to you.

Take advantage of today and live it the way you want to live it. Living it tomorrow or waiting until something else is different may just be too late.

"Don't live life in regret – live learning from your experiences"

Chapter 2

Health Basics

When you are healthy, you are seen and your energy felt to be a comfortable, joyful, energized satisfied and happy character radiating with positive energy.

A healthy person, is healthy from within, the strength and energy flowing from way deep down inside - so by the time this positive energy leaves the body, it has effected everything positively on it's way out and the person is left looking and feeling radiant.

The opposite of health is dis-ease, - displayed by a colorless, gloomy, tired exhausted and de-energized character representing negative energy. The root of it being again, deep down inside. The root is so bad because it is not being "fed" with the right "diet" in the human case positive energies and love, the " human-tree " cannot sprout and grow.

What happens in the process is that it starts to drain all the (water / nutrients) energy from everything close by, searching for "health", until it is draining every little bit from the outermost layers reaching out with ever thinner growing roots in an attempt to survive - leaving the person looking weathered, exhausted, aged, dry and without vitality or energy.

It is said that health is a state of mind. The implication being, that if you have your mind set on a "what is good for me" attitude, you will ensure that your body is looked after and treated correctly. This in turn ensures good health. Simple...almost!

The down-fall of this theory is that many people fail to include that the emotional and psychological aspect of health as covered by "Holistic Health Therapists", dealing with the body, mind and soul of an individual and this effect on health. To set your mind to the body, mind and soul aspect, you need to understand the way in which it works.

Follow me on this:
Take an orange tree and plant it in the desert. Would this be ideal? No, the tree would not survive the dry conditions.

In the same way, take a cactus and plant it in the arctic climate, this too would not work, it would freeze, the climate being too cold. But, if you plant the orange tree in a subtropical climate, and the cactus in the desert both will thrive as the conditions are ideal and suitable.

Back to our body, mind and soul. For your body cells to regenerate and grow healthy, they as the plants need "ideal" conditions. As the plants, humans also need: sun (warmth) air (oxygen), atmospheric pressure, water and food (energy source) in order to survive. All living organisms need these 5 elements for survival - directly or in-directly in a healthy quantity and of good quality.

Given that all 5 elements are present and available in abundance, we have survival and growth of healthy cells. But, in our lives we have factors, which affect the 5 elements and our body functions, which in turn affect the generation of healthy cells and regeneration.

Pollution on a global level, plus our personal air pollution including: smoking, body-sprays, sprays, pesticides, herbicides and other chemicals we use on a daily basis within our living environment - and still we expect our body to work properly, as well as the mental stress. There needs to be less pollution surrounding us on all levels of body, mind and soul for a cleansing process to take place.

Going into the 5 elements in a little more detail will give us the opportunity to understand this more clearly.

Sun (Warmth)
We need the warmth and the light coming with it for our metabolic processes (converting) and to help regulate our life cycle from day to night, work to rest.

But at the same time, the sun we are receiving in most parts of the planet, (due to the holes in the ozone layer caused by pollution) is too hard on our bodies, causing harm if over-exposed. In some areas on the planet, the sun due to the pollution can hardly be seen or felt through all the smog.

When we are angry, irritated or frustrated we too generate a tremendous amount of unnatural heat causing organism processes to speed up, over-work, over-heating the system.

Air
Oxygen, without it none of our life maintaining processes could function, we would not survive. Oxygen helps to release energy from our food cells. But we need good quality air for our bodies to function effectively and efficiently. With the continual cutting down of the rain forests and other natural vegetation, the emissions from the factories and the millions of cars daily on the planet, the quality of the oxygen has already gone from bad to worse, and continues to decline for which there is no end in sight to all the polluting.

Let us turn to our individual lives. How many people smoke and how many others are passive smokers, inhaling the smoke from a smoker nearby?

Have you thought of your child, or the other persons child that you are pushing in a pram in the streets, the baby breathing in all the gas from the cars in the highest concentration possible, being so low down and exposed. As a parent who smokes - are you aware of the ill health that you are passing on to your child? All this and we still expect our bodies to function normally.

Pressure
We need this for respiration, but by living under strain and "stress" we create false pressure within ourselves, causing confusion for the respiratory mechanics and not allowing us to breath strain-free. But we

still expect our bodies to function normally. The false pressure creates a situation where the body will not be getting a full dose of "fresh" air to replenish the body cells on each breath, and also not remove the carbon dioxide from the body on each breath, s creating only limited body functioning. Are you feeling tired, strained, exhausted - try breathing in a few really big healthy breaths of air and see how you will pick up .... think of the benefits of doing this daily!

Water
Unless you are lucky living with spring water well on your property, you are likely to be drinking lots of chemicals, especially chlorine. Even people living in the country with their own water are likely to have it contaminated, be it from a chemical spill from a factory, or the chemical fertilizers used nowadays from the local farmers - the chemicals dissolving and seeping into the water- table, directly flowing into your well or the river nearby is contaminating you. Water plays an important transport role in the body, and also a cleansing role.

As our body is made up of 80% water we can clearly see how important it is for our entity. Water also helps with the cleansing of the system.

Think how much water you put in a sink to wash up a few dishes, or flat plates, or how much you use to rinse out your coffee mug - now think how much water you drink everyday to wash the inside of your body? Many of us do not drink nearly enough water; rather pour coffee, tea, cokes or alcohol into ourselves.... And still expect our bodies to go on effectively and efficiently. One should try to drink about 8 glasses or 2 liters a day.

Food
This is an interesting one. Basically food is the substance from which the source of energy comes to keep the body functions working. But, gone are the days of nuts, seeds, grains, fruits, roots and vegetables - natural products only.

Today our bodies have to deal with colorants, flavorings, preservatives, and flavor enhances, substitutes and more chemically based ingredients. Most food is also over-cooked, and over-spiced, and our bodies must deal with completely unnatural situation. On top of all that, we mix all our foods and drinks when we have a meal in the wrong way and upset our digestive system even more - and still we expect the body to function normally!

So far we have read, in a very simple way that our bodies interact with the 5 elements - as best as they can in our modern world.

In the forthcoming parts of the book, we will take a look at how lifestyle affects the 5 elements and how that in turn influences our bodies on an ongoing basis.

Chapter 3

Material Assets or Invaluable Possessions?

Is your favorite material possession a teacup, a pen, a blanket, a key ring, perfume, a wardrobe, a car, a book, a plant, piece of jewellery or an antique?

What is your most prized and valuable possession - write it into the space below

_____

What would you go through if s something would be destroyed, damaged. Lost or stolen? How would you react, how would you feel about it? Write it into the space below

_____
_____

Could you replace it with another piece similar to the one/s in mind and be contented with that replacement? If yes, then it is more likely that you are not attached to material possessions, if you disagree - then read on.

Being unable to replace the item/s either means: you cannot get it anymore, or the sentimental value has turned it into a priceless "irreplaceable" possession.

Think of 20 other items in your living and working space.

1..
2..
3..
4..
5..
6..
7..
8..
9..

10...
11...
12...
13...
14...
15...
16...
17...
18...
19...
20...

Are you cluttering your life with material assets, priceless possessions, and irreplaceable possessions?

Material assets are things that you buy and use because everyone else has them and they service your needs, then when it's done doing what you bought it for you throw it out like a used tissue.

Or is your space cluttered with items that you could not replace nor ever get rid of? They take up space they cannot be used for very much in particular and normally take up more space than you really have, collecting dust, while standing on a shelf or lying in a box in the attic or in the garage and is only seen when someone else finds it and wants to throw it out.

This is usually when you say how much it means to you and that it is so special and cannot be thrown out. Needless to remind you that as special as you make it out to be, you have had it ignored in a box for months or even years since it was last "found".

Don't get me wrong, antiques are antiques and are collected as such and yes, I know that for collectors, one man's garbage it another mans gold. However, antiques you look at and have as apart of the furnishings if you are a collector.

But let me move on with this. The point is not the value of the possession or how old it is, but how attachment to these things plays havoc with your mind and life.

Very few people other than the millions who have been displaced or who have lost their homes know the lesson available to them here. The lesson is, that these possessions are just useful or "nice-to-have" things for our pleasure - but that they can be replaced

Think of someone living in the USA - of someone living in a luxurious surrounding, having lots of money and all that goes along with it.
Imagine this person owning their "dream" car -, a very expensive European sports car. Imagine that some hooligan scratches this car.

What will the person do? Does the owner go into a fit because his beautiful, priceless possession is ruined and it is the end of the world for him? Or does he simply shrug his shoulders, and take his car to the garage to get it fixed, without much to-do because although it is an inconvenience - he can well afford the insurance?

Do you know one of the few people or anyone who would react in the second way? It may not be a car; it may be a dress or a prized trophy, perhaps a pair of shoes too!

On the other end of the scale, a person in rural India. He does not have an expensive European sports car, or possibly any car, but he has a special teacup. If the cup were to be broken, this person will be just as affected in either of the ways described above, as the rich American with a scratched sports car.

Attachment is attachment - we all put a price tag on things we love. If we focused on life and ourselves we would realize that a teacup could be a favorite but at the end of the day it is still only a teacup.

Go now and look about your house for all of those items that no longer serve a purpose in your life, and throw them out, to make space for those you do need.

"Be grateful while you have got it and let it go when it is gone."

Chapter 4

Frustration Meets Love

Dis-ease and illness can come from " FRUSTRATION " in one form or another. There are many various types of frustration: mental, physical, emotional, spiritual, and sexual…but they are all frustration. Frustration is the inability to move forward due to personal bias on the topic where your frustration actually lies.

With this we can say that nearly everyone is suffering on some level - fathers, mothers, boys, girls, husbands, wives, priests, sisters, managers, sales personnel - all because the focus of their lives is not Love based, but on achievement. Many people are focusing on their place in society, their group, their community within the family, or amongst a group of friends as to how well they are doing, instead of on how happy and content they really are.

When a man feels attracted to a woman and a woman feels attracted to a man and when these two people are united in sexual passion due to the overwhelming feeling of Love, their attraction for this material world is realized as fake -beauty compared to the world within which they are emotionally enveloped - their world of Love.

Love and self-love in particular are the true key elements to success on your journey. You are not being promised wealth in the form of jewels, gold or money; but you are being offered peace of mind and an awakened consciousness with which you can act upon to assist in you achieving your goals.

Love is a very positive element, which has different effects on different people. Some people cannot sleep without being close to the one they love, others fly around the world only to be close to or with the ones they love. Mothers' will put their lives in risk because of the love they have for their children. Some people die when the one they love leaves them or have died - not feeling able to live without that love they shared with that person.

It is a bond so special although we cannot physically touch or see it - but when we feel it - we know we have got it, because nothing compares to that power of Love.

There are many common sayings that we can use and have been used for many years like:

- o Broken-hearted
- o Cold-hearted
- o Warm-hearted
- o Gentle-hearted
- o A caring heart
- o A heart of gold

.... And I am sure that there is many more like those.

Love can also be so painful that it hurts. Two people in love, separated for some reason, feel hurt being apart from the person they share such a special, strong bond with.

It is common knowledge that people who have lived their lives together for many years as family or very close friends, will often die within days or weeks of the other simply because they have suddenly such a big piece of their heart missing, that they can no longer go on without it.

Animals are no exception; they become a part of us. Your love for that animal is felt on a day-to-day basis and especially when separated from your special pet for a time.

Love has no boundaries or limitations - people have love for a town, place, an area, a teddy bear, a blanket, a musical instrument, a piece of clothing, a type of person, it is special and very powerful in many usual and unusual ways.

Love also stretches across most "normal" boundaries such as: between humans, plants, trees, material possessions (car, house) and lets not forget those pets, and even animals of different species have been studied as being so close due to the love they share - cats and dogs, goats and sheep; mice and cats.

The energy emitted through a "LOVE" person is so high that only positive energy can be around this person. It is so strong that anything negative will be repelled should it get near to the person.

What happens is, that the negative rises to the level of the positivity, which has a greater effect. Once it is positive, the negative pattern is lost and the energy of that will become positive.

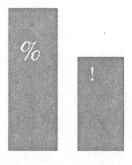

FIG 1   FIG 2

What you are going to learn in more detail in the chapters to follow is how self-love can change your life around completely for your own well-being and those around you.

If you want to build a house, solid foundations are a good start and then build on top of that. In life we too need a foundation called " Self- Love" - and on this we can build up our life, without it being blown over by a hurricane or cracking up due to use extreme use.

Through the course of this book you will learn how far a good dose of "mind-full living" can go if you get your first formula correct. You will grow and develop into yourself from living in what might feel like an unsettled world at the moment, to the fulfillment of living with Love and being at peace in the world /environment that you chose to surround you - because it will be your chosen one.

"The power is in knowing makes living it that much easier"

Chapter 5

Advice or Advise

We know what we like and what we don't like, but all the same we go about asking other people's advice on the matter. What we are actually doing is asking another person to tell us what they think would be best for us.

Example:

In certain life situations people believe that they should only do what is considered the "norm" or acceptable by society and by keeping to this they believe that they will not be shunned by others for being "different" - really meaning: by being themselves by doing what they want to how they want to.

The fact is that people who are shunned or ridiculed for being different, shock the "normal" society by having dared to go against the "normal"......... of which they consider themselves part. But in actual fact, those people feel ashamed for not standing up and doing for themselves as the other person has done for him/herself - so, they ridicule the person for not staying "acceptable by society's standard" the way that they have. It sounds strange - but true!

Nearly all of us were in school at some stage facing homework, exams, tests, or even home projects.

It could be guaranteed that at least some of the students would put their hearts into the work being undertaken for maximum achievement.

And then there are the others who would do barely enough for the project to be completed.

Last but not least, those who left it to the night before, or even bother to hand anything in.

After considering this, now think of those who would be the ones to do the bulling and teasing the ones who actually did the work properly!!

Compliments would be nice, but that would mean that the "lazy" student/s must admit that someone else has put in more effort than himself or herself. It also means that if someone else could put in a reasonable effort in the same time-span, then so could they have.

Remember that, by doing your own thing is important because sometimes the people around you feel themselves that it is too much work so will try and prevent you from doing it, and making them look bad. When you take on advice like this it is suiting their needs and not yours.

So you see, advice is something that we should ask of ourselves. Opinion is when we take another person's view into consideration, but this is only to help you get a feel of how people might respond, not a reflection on what to do or not to do.

Only you know what you really want. Ask yourself and be honest about it. Allow yourself to feel for the answer and you will get the right answer. Then ask yourself, "Is this a situation which is going to make everyone else pleased with that which I am doing, or is it really what I am looking for to make myself happy, without worrying about the reaction of the others?"

If your want or need includes: bodily harm, damage to yourself or others, violence or breaking the law in any way - all this could result in a tragic outcome, so don't go that way. But, if it is peaceful, nobody being physically hurt, injured and laws are not being broken, then you are on the right pathway!

LIVE LIFE LIKE A BUMBLEBEE

This goes hand in hand with what you believe and how you apply those beliefs to your life

To make yourself more confident in your choices, the next part we go into is Beliefs, which will enable you to see where you are actually coming from and how much affect your environment is having on you.

Chapter 6

Beliefs

A belief is your point of view on certain aspects. You accept and acknowledge a theory, a story, incidence or method put forward to you.

To believe "something" to e the truth, means that you accept that as the truth, by your natural judgment or by proof of it's working. You can also believe or disbelieve "that something" by the way it is put across or not. We may also believe that there are other possibilities to "the something". When this is the case, other possibilities mean that by not setting a restriction on whether you believe it or not.

A few examples:
The Wright brothers believed that it could be possible to fly similarly to birds. They did not think it impossible, so set to work on ways to fly. Many friends, colleagues and family members shunned and ridiculed them for attempting the idea they had. The brother's stuck with their belief and continued in spite of the negativity surrounding them, even although their family felt embarrassed by the idea.

Today we have the Wright brothers to thank for aviation the way we know it. Their original idea has since taken us into space and assisted us to travel faster than the speed of sound! How many times has an aeroplane taken you to a holiday destination or business trip - that was their IDEA that you were sitting in? They believed in themselves, and when you fly anywhere -it means you believe in their idea too!

Another believer in himself: Albert Einstein. He was known as a "Nutty Professor" with really unacceptable theories and concepts at the time he was researching them. He too was ridiculed, put down and laughed at! Now, all these years' later scientists and mathematicians constantly use his formulae and theories. He too believed in himself, his theories and concepts - and has since been accepted as accurate (many, many years later).

Many people believed in many different things since man came to this planet. Each of those beliefs has helped create the planet on which we live.

Be it the wheel, the chair we sit on, the paper we read off, the glasses we drink from, the car that transports us, the pen we write with, computers, radios, television - everything. A person who believed in himself and his idea/s created each one of these items.

In this way over decades - generations of people have evolved with their ideas to improve their life and those around them.

Is that not that what you want too? Improve your life?

So, take your ideas and make them work for you. They do not have to work for anyone else but you! Someone else's ideas will work for other people and yours for certain other people. If the group that is closest to you does not appreciate the idea - don't worry - they simply may not be ready for it yet, but go for it.

When your ideas fulfill and inspire you -they make you feel good about yourself; then those people around you will be happy to be there with you being in this positive frame of mind, rather than being depressed or frustrated, and grumpy because you are living a life you don't feel comfortable in.

"It takes more courage to change than it does to stay the same"

Chapter 7

Relationships Of Understanding

You don't have to be married to be in a relationship. A relationship is a co-existence between yourself and another "thing". It could be your dog, cat, plants, friends, neighbors, family, partner, lover, therapist or postman.

The two-way exchange is a give and take scenario, with plants you give them attention, water plant food, light and clean air, and they will grow, flower and decorate your home or garden -not to forget they clean the air and the flower gives off a lovely pleasant fragrance.

Pets that are treated well, loved and respected and given the attention they need will in return give love, respect, security, company and loyalty -priceless!

Help your neighbors where you can, be friendly and keep up a good co-existence. You never know when you may need to count on them for a cup of sugar, a ride into town or a helping hand when one is needed, however don't put yourself out trying if it is a one way relationship- it's meant to be an unconditional and fair exchange.

Treat others with the same dignity and respect that you would like to be treated with. Not only will the positivity make you feel good, but also it will keep you in a positive light by others around you. Rather be liked than disliked - it does not cost anything extra.

At the same time, this is about being yourself rather than who other people might expect you to be. By being who they expect you to be, you are making their life a pleasure whilst you are not having any fun. Why concentrate on making someone else's life a pleasure when you could be focusing that energy on making your own life a pleasure, and let them do the same for themselves!

"If you can't love yourself the way you are, then you can't expect anyone else to love you that way"

When you are having a bad day, and don' tell anyone – they will treat you normally. When you are having a bad day and say that everything is fine, when people ask – it is not fair to become angry with them later because they are not being sensitive enough.

"Be Open, Honest and Disregard the rest" – tell it like it is. If your system tells you that you are good, then say so, if your system tells you that you are not feeling great or the best then say that too.

Many people get caught up in not sharing how they feel, but if you are not sharing how you feel, then how is anyone supposed to know? Not everyone can read minds and NO – partners don't know how you are because they are your partner. In relationships what you put in is what you get out, as is with most things in life.

How well do you know your partner or best friend or even family member? Do you know their favorite: color, food, artist, place, plant, car, pet hate, moment, parents names, sport, pet, ... so do you? If not you need to find out, and if you do, well then you are on the right path within that relationship, but how much of that do they know of you?

Your family might keep on buying you socks or jumpers or a new hat or the same thing that they get you every year... because you don't tell them, and if you have told them and they still keep on buying these items, then you did not make yourself clear enough, or they may be getting old and forgetful, so just change it.

"If you want to be accepted as who you are, then first accept yourself the way you are."

Chapter 8

Assumption

As far as I am concerned, assumption is the mother of all problems. We have all been through experiences that we can hold directly responsible to assuming that:

The other person was going to pay the bill
The other person was going to stop at the intersection
The other person was going to do the dishes
The other person was going to vacuum the house
The other person was going to fetch the kids from school.
The other person would do what you have done in the past
The other person would do something because you hinted at it.
The other person would buy the lottery ticket this week
And so on.........

No, no, no, - don't ever assume unless it is for research purposes and it is something hypothetical and will not have a real physical result... in Britain a few weeks ago a couple won a Lottery draw worth about £5 million, but he did not get the ticket assuming that his partner would get it ... ouch! That must have hurt him, and probably will for quite some time.

I am not going to ponder on other areas in which we can assume, except into the relationships area.

When the word relationship is used it is to be used to describe what I have with you, what you have with your dog or cat, you mother, aunt, uncle, myself and my pony, father, sister, brother, boss, neighbor, neighbor's dog, plants, in short - practically anything you feel you have a relationship or an interaction with.

LIVE LIFE LIKE A BUMBLEBEE

To get you into focus, I am briefly going to give you a few more examples on why not to assume in relationships.

Let's use the neighbor's dog:

You have lived side by side for many years, you have always visited next door and you and the dog get on well.

You are playing ball with your child and the ball lands in the neighbor's garden. You assume that the dog knows you well enough to let you in on "his" property although his master / mistress is not there.

When reaching the front gate, you are being greeted by the dog, which is wagging his tail. You greet him and proceed to open the gate.

The dog stops waging his tail and a deep growl comes from his throat. He does not want to let you in, because that is what he instinctively knows when his master is not around - protect his territory.

You realize that your assumption was wrong and that for the time being, the ball will have to stay where it is, and a well-mannered and controlled RETREAT is in order.

That was simple enough, right? Most of us have done this at some time or other in our lives.

I see it over and over again in my work with: my clients of both sexes, married, lovers, colleagues, hetero-and homosexual couples, best friends- and it is always the same. Everyone assumes what the other person might or might not be doing, feeling, looking at, or talking about, thinking about, pointing at, sniggering about, saying, expressing, or not expressing and similar assumptions.

Let us go to your work place.

At work you "feel" that people in the office are (always) talking about you behind your back, they are seemingly looking in your direction, possibly even pointing in your direction.

Do you know 100% for sure that all this is directed at you?
That they are talking about you?
That they are laughing at you?
That they are looking at you poorly?

Have you considered that they might not be directing their attention at you at all, but happen to be standing talking, not wanting others to hear a personal conversation? And so are keeping an eye on their surroundings?

What makes you so sure that they are really talking about you? And if they are talking about you - maybe it is really something nice, compliments about your clothing for instance. Or your outfit reminded them of some incident or another person. Don't see it in a negative light right away – that's assuming.

Are they really laughing at you? Is it not possible that they are sharing a joke? Could they not perhaps only be looking to see your reaction, as they might be aware that they are laughing out a bit loud, or the joke was crude or. or .. or ... or a multitude of possibilities.

You feel they look down at you? Why? Could this not be a sign of insecurity? What if they really they must admire you, your work, your clothes, your personality, your success, and are not sure how to approach you?

There are hundreds of different explanations that would fall in with these examples, but what is important, is to see and realize that when one assumes, one usually focus's on the negative possibility.

Human nature is such that we seldom look to the good of another, but rather to the negative side of things.

In the examples the person could have been getting compliments from colleagues, but we have the tendency to assume that when someone says something in our presence that we can't hear - it's about us and it must be negative.

Another day-to-day example involves couples. Couples have a tendency to assume what their partner thinks about them or how they will react to situations. And what is and what is not wanted.

A Relationship is not about 2 people playing hit-and-miss as to what your partner is after and what not. Relationships are like plants: they need nourishment, oxygen, sunlight, water and a good environment in which to grow strong. It is important to find out from your partner what sort of nourishment or environment they need to thrive in, and also when and under what conditions they may need to change.

If you like a cup of tea, will you assume that your partner also wants tea and bring a cup without making sure? Or are you simply going to ask if they'd like some tea? Like this you learn what you like and what they like, and at what regularity they like certain things. Sometimes too much of a good thing is a bad thing, so ask to make sure first – you will find out soon enough.

Routines and habits come along to stay with couples that have been together over a longer period of time. Going out for example may have somehow ended up to be a Friday night "must" for him. Although "she" would like to go out more than once a week, she assumes that "he" is too tired from a hard weeks work and won't break the routine. "He" however, would also like to break the routine and go out more, more often, but "he" too assumes that "she" does not feel like it.

See how easily something like this can happen through poor communication due to assuming too much. This could be a happy couple, but instead, they are starting to resent one another because of what they are assuming of one another when there is absolutely no need

– just open your mouth speak your mind so others know what is going on in there.

Ask and you shall receive! There are only 2 answers: yes or no. Speak, ask, then it will be clear and you won't feel lousy un-necessarily because of what you assume your partner does or does not want.

If you get an answer you did not "want" to hear, discuss it thoroughly or try something different. But do not give up. A fresh approach could work wonders on both parts.

ASS-U-ME
"By assuming you make an ass of u and me!"

Chapter 9

Intuition

What is it? How does it work? And can we really count on it?

Intuition is said to be the little voice that you hear inside your head telling you what you should or should not do...an advice of some sort.

Where does it come from? Who knows? It can't be proven scientifically. So for some it is information from the "Universal Information Library" or "channeled " messages from a spiritual guide, and for some it is simply a "gut feeling".

I believe that as with animals of nature, which also have to make choices for survival - to do or not to do, theirs is called instinct, and so too do I believe that our intuition is a *great part* of our instinct.

Your subconscious is sending out signals. It is your decision as to where you feel that this Intuition comes from, but do yourself a favor - USE IT!

Most of us have been told at some time or the other to: "trust your intuition", "listen to yourself for the answer ", or "follow your instinct". In all of these cases - the thing to actually do would be to follow the lead of the "reaction" you feel at the time and circumstance.

However ... If it were a decision that needs to be made on the spur of the moment - "follow your gut" would be the well-told choice ...... but ...

You may or may not have been in such a circumstance, that the pressure of the situation may very well cause you to make a "rash" decision (by not having looked ahead at that deciding moment for possible outcomes), the effect of this "follow your gut" reaction could be disastrous on a more permanent basis. So-unless it's a "life or death" response - don't make rash decisions, but take your time and think about it, including the knock on effect down the road or in a few weeks or even a few years.

Intuition is being and responding naturally to a situation that comes up.

If you are emotional, stressed, anxious, depressed, scared - STOP and contemplate a logical response before you resort to doing a "spur of the moment" thing, which may end up disastrous! But, if you are calm, relaxed and not off-balance or feeling threatened in any way, then respond intuitively!

For too long now we have been putting ourselves through torment.

For too long, we (being nearly all of us) have been told to do what we feel is right at the time, to be instinctive.

For too long now we have been taking the long road, full of extra bumps to trip over, and pot holes to fall into - instead of being able to take the short, straight and flat road taking us directly to our destination.

It is time to start thinking. Up till now most of us have done that intuitive thing to get us out of a situation - but now we need to learn an alternative route.

Feelings and emotions are temporary - changing from one moment to the next, as the circumstances change. A rash thought may cause detours along an otherwise straight road - but if we learn to focus, then we can move on to a more positive place.

Think before you react. Take time to breath, think, focus on the question and possible results before you answer rationally with your well being, self-preservation and personal development in mind.

"The moment may last forever – so consider it thoroughly first"

Chapter 10

The Wheel of Life

In actuality it is YOUR circle of LIFE, because you are the focus of the wheel and the different areas of your life make up the focus. To begin with we take the wheel:

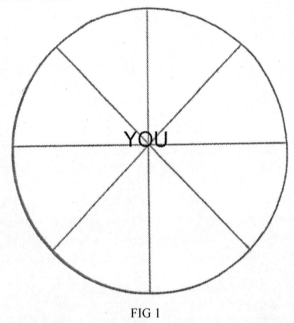

FIG 1

Why a wheel, you may ask? Well - what is a wheel and how does it work, and this will be the answer.

A wheel is a frame, round with no start and no end, held in that shape by a supporting structure of spokes from the center to the circumference, with a rubber tire over the top to absorb the bumps along the way.

Now place yourself in the center of the wheel.

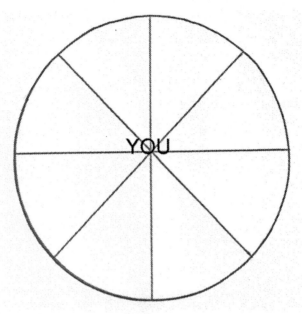

FIG 2

What does this mean? It means that you are the support system of the circle, all of the spokes holding it together.

The next step is to recognize the rim of your wheel as your environment and everything within it, both past and present - those elements that make you the person you are today.

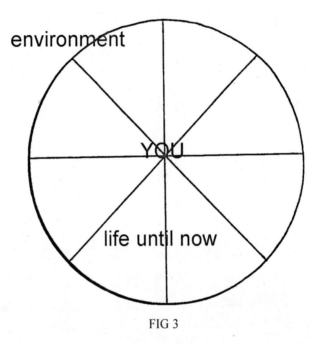

FIG 3

Your life environment consists of all and everything that has happened in your life up to this moment in time. Your childhood, family, friends, education, travel, pets, jobs, partners, assets- absolutely everything you can think of, so put them into a wheel.

FIG 4 – Barman, Waiter, Military, Driver, Cook, Reflexology, Massage.
Iridology

Here would an early example of my own wheel, so you can see what I
mean by putting in the different areas of your life. These are just a few
things that I was doing with regards to work and "career" , but the next
wheel breaks up my life in to the normal elements that make up ones life.

You may find areas of your life that are not a part of mine, so feel free to
add in as many spokes as suits your life.

FIG 4a – Education, Equipment, Friends, Pets, Family, Good in Life, Work, Possessions, Travel, Achievements, Health, Activities, Partners, Bad in Life, Hobbies, Cars

The bigger you make the wheel, the more you can fit in. But to start off with, draw small ones writing in what and with whom you have this in your life.

This is the easiest as most people know the people around them, and where they fit into their lives.

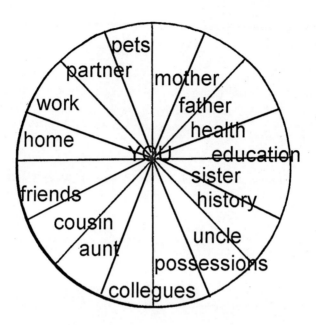

FIG 5 –Mother, Health, Father, Education, Sister, History, Uncle, Possessions, Aunt, Colleagues, Cousins, Friends, Other Cousin, Pet, Job, Home

Then with time you can make up a separate wheel for each of these areas in your life. Look at your wheel and look at all of it in as much detail as possible and comprehend all that you have in your life. So my work wheel might look very similar to that in Fig 4 a few pages back.

Your past has created your present-day reality and the wonderful person that you are.

All of these life factors keep your wheel moving forward and so your life. If you have a problem going on, a particular issue bothering you - write it in to your wheel if you have not done so, then look at your wheel again and look at your issue. Focus on what you want for yourself. Is it worth dropping everything else and stopping your life for one thing?

Or is there enough support (spokes) to keep you supported without that one spoke?

FIG 7-1 FAMILY 8 members including YOU + Uncle FRED

Look at FIG 7-1; this is your life before the issue with your UNCLE FRED came up.

Then your issue came up with a particular person, so go to into your wheel, and if the issue is affecting your FAMILY then write that down alongside your wheel to keep your mind on track.

Ask yourself about the issue "can I move forward with this while I work through it, or is it in my best interest to drop the issue?"

To get that answer, cover up the "person" or issue-causing factor, which in this case is UNCLE.

FIG 7.2 FAMILY WITHOUT UNCLE FRED

What you have is 8 parts of your LIFE affecting your FAMILY in a positive way and 1 part in a negative way. Either you try to work through it or you leave it behind you and take the lesson with you, not the issue.

When you have a problem with a person or thing, if you cannot solve it right away, which is the best thing to do, then simply distance yourself from that particular issue, and if it happens to be a person, then give yourself the space from that person, until you can work it out, before you say or do something that you may regret due to the emotional side of things.

Try and complete your wheel, and all the little ones that will make up your life, then each year redo the areas where you feel changes have taken place, or redo the entire system is that much better to refresh and keep in touch with your environment.

"It takes more courage to change, than it does to stay the same"

Chapter 11

I Am Listening and I Hear You.

How often have you found yourself sitting with that dull feeling over your body with a glossy and unfocussed eyes while you gawk unmoved at the person opposite you, but you do not hear their words because your thoughts are in a different topic in a different place?

Honestly - I have on occasion found myself doing exactly that. Normally this will happen if the person talking to you would be on a topic of no interest whatsoever to you, so you lose interest quickly and your mind escapes the boredom to thoughts of something that would be of interest to you..... Or perhaps memories of the wild party last night at your friends place.

It was along the journey whilst moving into the world of Alternative Health that I learned the importance of listening and how to remain focused. The importance of listening and the necessity to be able to respond to the speaker in a way that the speaker feels heard is so important!

Many people in conversation respond with the proverbial: "aha", "mmm", "ok", "I see", "yeah" and "yup".

We all want to be heard at some time. It may not be now, it may be in 2 months from now, but sometime the need may arise where you may need to be heard - someone to talk to who can listen while you expresses yourself. Don't count yourself out. It could be anything from dissatisfaction in the workplace, a troubled relationship, expression of emotions (depression) to being able to tell someone that you had the best day of your life, or hopefully not - your worst day.

The topics range from anything to everything, lasting from 30 seconds, to 30 minutes or even perhaps 3 hours of your time.

If time is a problem and you would like to be there for the person, then being honest by telling them that you have another scheduled event, but would be happy to continue another time. Even better would be to advise professional Counseling or Therapy that which best suite their needs.

If it is someone you know - this may be the biggest moment in their life, because they may have been holding on to this for many years and you may be the only person that they feel that they can talk with.

But you will know if there is something wrong, when it is someone close, so if they seem "off" and unsettled, try and make a few extra minutes to hear them.

Listening to people on a professional level or not, one should take in to consideration the following:

You are not listening to me when:
You are looking straight past me, while I am talking to you.
You do not care about me.
You say you understand before you have heard or know me enough after a few minutes.
You have an answer for my problem before I have finished telling you what my problem is.
You cut me off before I have finished speaking.
You finish off my sentences for me.
You interrupt me, and start talking about something completely different.
You find me boring and let me feel it.
You feel critical of my grammar, accent and vocabulary.
You are dying to tell me something.
You tell me of your experience making mine seem unimportant.
You are communicating to someone else in the room.

You are listening to me when:

You look at me while I am talking.

You come quietly into my private world and let me be me.

You really try to understand me even if I am not making much sense.

You grasp my point of view even when it is against your convictions.

You allow me the dignity of making my own decisions even though you may think they could be wrong.

You do not take my problem from me, but allow me to deal with it in my own way.

You hold back your desire to give me good advice.

You do not offer me religious solace.

You give me room for myself to discover what is really going on.

You accept my gift of gratitude by telling me how good it makes you feel to know that you have been helpful.

"Every person you ever meet, will have an influence on you as you have on them, so look to what is being offered"

Chapter 12

The Closer, The Harder?

Friends and family make it that much harder. Today and as it was centuries ago, there are families, communities, groups, organizations and cultures which all have issues.

From the Royal family of one country right down to the "normal" person, problems and issues have no gender or race preference - but what you can count on is at least a taste of it at some time in your life.

Some of you may be asking, "What of those who do not have family?"

Think about it, you grew up somewhere, did you not?   Even if you grew up in an orphanage, or with grandparents, relatives or foster parents - which would have been your "family" at the time being, there would certainly have been rivalry of some kind!

Sooner or later you could find yourself in a situation where your "family member" is doing something or even everything you dislike or find offensive.

This person is special in some way to you, how is the person going to react if you tell them how you feel? They most probably do not see themselves as you do. The situation may even become worse when mutual acquaintances may also have noticed this offensive behavior and are saying poor things about your "family members" bad habit.

You know that to inform the "family member" will be hard but important, and that the "family member's" first reaction will be, defense, and then attack, which is a common sign of insecurity.

If what you tell them was not true it is likely that the "family member's" response would be to joke and laugh at the accusation, although sometimes this on its own is a form of cover-up.

So the person, who defends by attacking as a way of response, is the person more likely in denial, although on a deeper level be aware of how they really are - but will want to hide it.

When someone has been doing something for a long time, it becomes a habit, or second nature and becomes a part of his or her character. When this happens they no longer remember it as a habit but as something they have always done.

The hard part is getting someone to understand and see what he or she is doing through another people's eyes. Think of how you may feel if a close friend (or family member) approached you to inform you that not only were your manners were atrocious and offensive, but your nose picking habit was also the talk of the town.

Your reaction upon hearing this would be either:
1. Shock and/or disbelief
2. Perhaps laughter
3. Defense

Shock and /or disbelief could well be because someone has finally spoken out against them or shock that you have a bad habit which you were not aware of although everyone else was, and even that people take notice of what they may be doing.

Laughter - said to be the best medicine...perhaps they do need healing of some sort. The laughter is the opposite reaction to shock - here the person takes it as a silly joke - nobody would take something so "small" so serious or to not want to believe that which is being told to them. They realize it was not quite the proper thing to have done or said but they did not think anyone would be watching or listening that carefully enough to be offended.

Defense - brings a military picture into mind - something being attacked needs to be defended. So, the defense reaction may indicate that the person is feeling attacked by these insinuations about poor behavior or whatever they are being accused of.

This type of person is likely to be rigid in their thinking and will find it difficult to comprehend constructive criticism, but instead see it as a blatant attack or abuse of their character.

Bearing in mind what kind of response your reaction may draw, you will need to be prepared for all 3 circumstances, with words of meaning said with sincere compassion.

One more response would be acknowledgement. That is when the person knows they have been doing things out of line that was likely to offend or hurt others, but circumstances at the time and their mental status did not cater for the needs of others. These people will usually be apologetic and sincere about it, possibly asking for some guidance of some sort. "Easier said than done" I can hear you saying. In some cases it is not easy.

At the end of the day you have got to ask yourself these questions:

- How am I going to feel if this situation gets worse and I know I could have said or done something, but didn't?
- Is what I have to say for the well -being of the other person?
- Is what I have to say true, and do I know this without doubt?
- Is anyone other than the person involved going to be effected and is it good or bad?

Answer these questions truthfully and you will know if what you are about to do is the right thing.

There is a little motto that I live by when it comes to situations where family and good friends are involved, (and sometimes even applies to clients when appropriate) and that is: "If you can't be honest with the people closest you, then who else is ever going to be?"

In most cases family and friends will say things to keep the other happy, but what about the emotional things that can hurt for years at a time when they go wrong.

People do not like to upset any balance they may have within any relationship, even if it means being honest. So if friends won't be that honest with one another - than who will? When it comes to my family, I believe it not my right, but my duty to speak my mind on all issues where I feel that the other family member/s may not be seeing something, or I feel that they might get hurt. I know that if I do not say anything, as a blood relative - then there is an even better chance that nobody else will either!

I am prepared to hurt the feelings of those that I love by speaking my mind if I feel that it something that they need to be made aware of and will benefit and in no way harm them.

It is most important to let them know why I am saying that which I am saying, and also because I care, and would not say something to hurt them if it was not for their own benefit.

Being aware that we all need to make our own mistakes, some people will not take heed to anyone's advice - but when you feel someone needs to be exposed to certain information, then gently try get it across.

" You can take the horse to the water, but you can't make it drink "

Chapter 13

Are You Really Guilty?

It may be something you did or said which you feel will hurt a person close to you if they find out. It may have been last night, it may be something from last week, last month, last year, 2 years ago, 20 years ago or it may be from even further back than that. The incident/act may be something that you took part in, witnessed or have information on.

It could also be anything from: breaking your word, displeasing parents, a summer fling which should have never happened and your present partner does not know, seeing something private that you should not have and now view the people differently or breaking the law.

If it's the information group: does the information you have threaten your life in any way? Or that of another person? If yes, then you need to do what is right and get help from the right people. The police have confidential help lines, church, counselors, therapists all these people can help you or your information get to the right people, and to get the right sort of advice you need.

Information is free in most cases, available in many shapes and forms: books, cinema, video, lecture, study classes, courses, tales, stories, folk lore, life experience, exposure to an act or deed which all provide you with expected or unexpected information. The choice now would be what you would do with it - to use it or discard it!

Guilt is about remorse and shame. Talking about guilt is very difficult because it is acknowledging to yourself and another of something that in your own eyes should not have been done.

A guilty conscience after doing something you know you should not have done, but did anyway is one thing. Telling someone about it is another challenging but very easing on the mind

Perhaps you have met someone recently and are feeling guilty that they do not know "all" of your past, but you don't really want to tell them.

Ask yourself the following:

- Is this information going to change the person you are?
- Is this information going to cause bodily harm to anyone?
- Will your partner/ friend benefit or burden them by knowing about "it"?
- Does this information have any relevance to your partners / friends life?

If you can live with your past and it does not and will not affect your partner / friend directly in any way, then there is no need to tell them. If you feel you need to tell someone, then go to a therapist or a priest. Get it off your chest and get on with your life without this on your shoulders.

We all make "mistakes" at some time, but try and see them as "lesson opportunities" instead - lessons learned.

What you have is in the present - today. Make the most of each day and remember that your past (from the time of conception) created the person you are today, including things, which are stirring guilty feelings - the good and not so good have made you who you are now.

"You can change your past as much as you can affect it"

Chapter 14

Be Open, Honest & Disregard The Rest

Wow - what a statement and how do you expect to get away with that - I can hear your thoughts ringing loud.

The statement can be as loud or as subtle as you want it to be. But before you decide on that, it would be a good idea to put it into realistic perspective for you so it can be understood.

Being able to grasp a concept or to understand how it works takes away any complexity that may be experienced without this understanding.

The statement is something that came to me whilst studying and working at the Personal Development, a positively rewarding task when there is personal developing to be done - and there always is as it's an ongoing thing.

Personal Development is about doing work on the Self in ways, which would bring out the person that has been hidden from the world. Life out there in "civilized" society has unwritten rules, that we all somehow know and try to abide by, and which will make us as "normal" as the next person!

This is for people who are unable to reach within themselves for strength, to be what they are or want to be, or on the other hand, want to become more of who they feel they are.

Whether you fit into the above category or not it makes life a lot easier if you are: open, honest and disregard the rest of the nonsense that does not suit your needs.

What does BE OPEN, HONEST AND DISREGARD THE REST mean? Well, it's almost as it reads: be open, and honest and disregard the rest.

Before getting carried away, it is best that I get to the part about understanding the concept. Let us break it down.

"BE" is a way of saying, "exist", as it is, what it is. For who you are by just being naturally - YOU.

What about "OPEN"? A doorway, a free space, unhindered, no resistance, free flowing, as opportunity stands, not shut, not blocked.

"HONEST" - truthful, loyal to yourself and others, no falseness, the way it is, nothing hidden, nothing changed, what is true for you, what's real not made up?

"DISREGARD" - not to consider, ignore, distance, forget about, pay no attention, take no heed, not to listen, forget about, push aside if approached with.

"The REST" - everyone else, what's left over, other than yourself, the remainder, all other options not taken/chosen.

To try this out, make a sentence of each group: exist, unhindered, loyal to yourself and others and pay no attention to what's left over.

Be, who you are, or who you want to be - if that's whom you feel comfortable with.

Be open and honest about who you are, to yourself and others. How you are what you are, and what you are not. Say what you like and what you don't like. Say yes when you mean it and no when you mean it. Say what you want and what you don't want - don't leave space for incorrect interpretation.

Disregard the rest, does not mean "forget that other people exist", but in connection to the above it means disregard what others want for you or from you, if it means that they benefit and you don't'! It means follow your own heart and mind not what everyone around you likes or how he or she thinks - that would mean you would be living according to the way they think and not yourself.

We are all individuals we still differ from one another (except identical twins) in thoughts that influence and share your lives. Similarity is not "the same"!

Be that person who you always thought you were. Listen to the voices inside your head, be the one pushing you to what is best for you. Only you will know what is best for you - others may have had similar situations, but there can never be another the same as you.

This lifetime is only lived once, so make the most of each day. Every time you put something off, or delay it, is time wasted.

Do you really want to look back on the last day, month or year and wonder how different things might have been or be if you did them when you wanted to and how you wanted to?

So what can we do about this wonderful modern world in which we live? One thing I am NOT going to suggest is to stop buying into technology, because that is how the world is moving "forward". But I AM going to suggest: "buy" some time for yourself.

And in order to buy yourself some time, you need to purchase a diary...one, which breaks the day up into 30-minute slots, starting at about 7 am and ending about 8 pm.

Once you have the diary take charge of your life through time management. It is up to you to allocate time for your chores and your appointments - be fair but don't be soft about it. You need to make a commitment to yourself and in this way you will be able to reward yourself some time during the day or the evening, which you are to use for yourself only!

ANTHONY LYLE SMITH

Time for you, the family friends, work, sport, hobbies, chores, meetings, social gatherings, shopping and special occasions are all things that you should have in your appointment times, so that you have time allocated to everything in a fair and unburdening way.

Perhaps you want to use YOUR time to have a massage a bubble bath, to curl up and read, to meet a friend you haven't seen in ages,.....Your special time is for you to choose what it will be used for - nobody else must be allowed to influence it.

You can influence your future by making today as good as you want tomorrow to be, but you can't change or influence the past - but you can learn from it.

77

Chapter 15

The Pit Of Understanding

The Pit Of Understanding is a place that nobody can see, but at some time in nearly everyone's life - it is a place one can feel. Like Love, you know it when it hits you - also you will really know that you are in the pit.

The Pit however, does not feel nice, is not comfortable, feels lonely, there seems to be no way out, and feels like it is going to last forever. Being in the pit feels like you are living in your own soundproof fish-tank, where everyone can see you, but nobody can hear your "call" for help.

The Pit is a place where we will place ourselves for the purpose of personal growth and development. This may sound really weird, but once the concept is explained you will feel more comfortable with it.

The Pit Of Understanding works when you allow it to, and when you choose to be in it, instinctively knowing that something good will come from it.

By following the numbers in the diagram, you can follow your progress and after the explanations are complete, you will know exactly where you are in your life, and at which stage of your life-path you are.

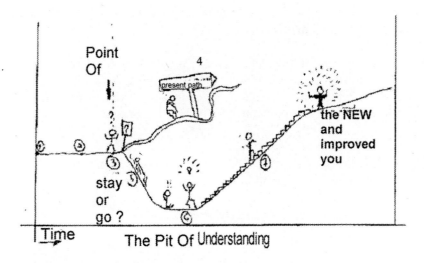

Point Of

4

present path

the NEW and improved you

stay or go ?

Time

The Pit Of Understanding

Starting at:

1

This represents your birth, and the first 10 or so years of your life - childhood. This is time whilst in your mother's womb and up until and including you're most educational years, in which one grows and develops into a personality, with the basic tools for life.

They are the most important years of life in terms of growth and development. It is in these years when the brain is so absorbing that development through encouragement to assimilate should take place from those around you, your elders. This also determines the characteristics, strengths, weaknesses - the more you know and are exposed to, the more confident you are likely to feel, considering that this educational phase of your life was supported and not shunned or hindered making you feel bad or guilty for having the knowledge.

It is in these first years that one learns ~ what is "good" and what is "bad", the things that you can and can't do, literature, writing, reading, eating, dressing, washing, hygiene, manners and being able to absorb and process information so that you can use it and develop as an individual - if that is not limited by those around you.

Is about taking the "individual" character moulded by those first 10 years and fine tuning them into everyday life capabilities, through puberty and the growth changes that go with it, to educational skills, and a specialist field on which you would like to earn your living one day.

2

Puberty is the image years, where the hormones do the thinking and talking, but again-if the individual has had exposure to information and matured, they will feel good about themselves, and this information will assist the person in being a more extravert character.

However the individual that has been kept and protected through the learning-experimenting-with-life years, is more likely to feel uncomfortable out of their own "space", making them more introvert in character. These are also the people who are more likely to be taking on the "stuff" of others, having not had the lessons to do their own thing, and more often for others.

3

Is usually the point in people's lives where they stop to reflect as to where they are, and where they are not. It is at this point where they either decide to change, or to simply go on with the life they have been living to this point.

It is from this point that people either move ahead with their own avenue on the learning curve for life, or continue to "do" for others and live a manipulated life in the hands of others, like a puppet on a string, with no or very little chance to think and "Do" for themselves.

4

Is the same life path direction, along the straight and narrow, no change - doing the same thing day in and day out, quite happy to go on the same way you have been up to that point in time. The opportunity to change faces you, but you decline the offer and go forward as you always have.

5

Once this is decided, and they decide to CHANGE, the "work and change" will begin to take place. Once this begins, it will feel like the life you once were living, is disappearing - and everything starts to feel strange... as you begin the descent into the pit.

The decision and choice to change will release the thoughts and ideas that were keeping you in the old space of: guilt, resentment, fear, anxiety, insecurity and regret. You will start to feel them - these are the emotions behind the reasons that helped you decide that you wanted to move on and change.

By making the choice to change, you have opened doors, which you previously kept closed to yourself, and all the thoughts and ideas, which you kept from yourself, will start popping up in your mind, stirring up all sorts of feelings, emotions, and questions about your past, present and future.

It is here that the new thought patterns and ideas start to challenge the old ones, which allow you to see the reasoning you gave for the old ones, which makes clear the want to change. These thoughts you are having are called "Understanding". The more new thoughts you have, and allow in, the more able you are to see yourself. This acknowledgement of your ways is the growth and development that takes place.

6

It is at this point when the empowerment begins to take effect. This happens when you start applying your new thought patterns and ideas to your life, and begin to feel the positivity coming from it as a result. You will begin to feel confident about yourself, good in what you are doing, and life will shine with a brighter light and greater meaning.

7

Through the changes, come understanding and growth opportunities. This personal development takes place at a new level of thinking, one on which you may have always dreamed of living, and now due to growth-full change - you can.

8

By the time you reach this point, you will be looking to yourself with Unconditional Love and Pride. This is when positive integration has become a constant subconscious occurrence. Similarly, as we learn to speak, add, or subtract - with time we also have to learn to think positively.

Once this has happened often enough, your brain will create this positive thinking as your new thought pattern, which will "naturally" be integrated from a subconscious level.

 The positive integration actually began as soon as you decided to change (3). From then on it has been an adventure of growth and development, training yourself into your new way.

At this stage of the adventure, you will be walking with a smile on your face, a spring in your step, and a positive outlook on life ahead. Your days will be filled with opportunities to learn, grow and develop; leading a challenging, growth-full and creative way with which to make your life and your interests exactly what you want them to become.

"Be who you are, not who others want you to be!"

Chapter 16

Stress

Stress, stress, and more stress...it's a word you hear everyday and by more and more people all claiming to be stressed!

I remember a time when only the "big-time" professionals were the stressed ones. People with lots of responsibility like: Doctors, Lawyers, Company Executives and not to forget our politicians.

Today however, it's the "young ones", not only the older ones who are suffering from stress.

As I have on many occasions before, I am going to say again: I do NOT believe in stress!

What? Why? I can hear you asking. Well - here's the answer:

By definition stress means: in mod use.

To subject (or person): to force, or compulsion, to constrain or restrain, overwork, fatigue. This is the basic definition of the word "stress" in all terms of voice, sound, and an object - all of which are on a physical level.

The "stress" we are talking about is that of: family, business, work, career, education - most of which the resulting forces acting within these environments is said to be stress. Read the words again - "to force, or compulsion, to constrain or restrain, overwork, fatigue". Interesting isn't it.

How do we classify stress by modern standards? Over-worked, under-paid, too much going on at one time, accounts to pay, "young ones" to look after, family matters, all these life stresses...and much, much more.

Think for a bit what you would consider to be stress in your life... try and find 5 possible stress factors (write them down).

1. _____
2. _____
3. _____
4. _____
5. _____

Read over that which you have written a few times, to think and feel how it affects you to think about those things.

- Think of how it affects you and how it makes you feel to think of these things?
- Do you feel good or not so good?
- Do you feel happy or saddened?
- Is your body relaxed or tense?
- Is your body at comfortable or uncomfortable?

In all likely hood you will be feeling the more negative of the options given.

Now for the best news in the world: YOU CREATED IT!! Yes, you did and now for the really, really good news - YOU, and only YOU have the power to get rid of it, because you and only you created it.

Stress is merely the symptom that has surfaced. Symptoms work like this: when your body is discomforted, the liver can't open it's mouth and say: "excuse me, would you stop loading me with toxins which I have to try and remove from the system?" It does not have a mouth so it will start sending messages in the form of e.g. a skin condition, giving you a hint that "something" is not right.

So, the symptom is merely the mail that the postman delivers. When you open the mail and read the bad news - you don't bash the postman as being the deliverer of the bad news, do you? He only delivered it. You would need to go to the person who wrote it. In other words: go to the source, the root!

Perhaps you ignored all the messages up until now, and now the postman brought a final reminder.... you have overdrawn your account again!!

YOU spent the money - Did YOU "pay" your account? Receiving a final reminder would mean that YOU did not; therefore by simple deduction it is YOUR own fault. YOU ignored the previous statements, and thought it would go away.... and YOU yourself are the reason for the "stress" it may be causing for you.

What if there are many accounts, you have not paid = more stress! YOU knew when YOU bought the goods that YOU should not have bought them because YOU could not afford to pay them off in the first place...YOU CAUSED YOUR OWN STRESS.

If YOU are being overworked .... are YOU being paid for it? If not, have YOU said something to YOUR management, spoken to YOUR representative or have YOU allowed this to happen, by not speaking up for YOURSELF, thereby being manipulated. Stress is NOT about people, it is a force put onto something, and was never intended to apply to people. Not taking up the responsibility for your own good when you should is not stress - it's silly. In today's modern society, people are too worried to speak up for themselves, or to say what they would like to say because "somebody" might not like it. Do you like it? No!

Then why should you be the one to suffer when there is no need to? So long as you keep putting up with other people's nonsense - they will keep giving it to you.

It's not about them - it's about you, and what is and what is not good for you. Being used by others, no matter who does the using -is not healthy! Speak up, take control in the moment and stop waiting for it to be over before you do something about it.

By then you are "stressed", and that is when you know you have allowed YOURSELF TO BE USED.

Think of an INBOX and an OUTBOX. Even get yourself two boxes for your desk. Work to be done goes into the INBOX, and work done goes into the OUTBOX.

If you are STRESSED it simply means that YOU are not clearing work from the INBOX and suddenly there is a whole load that needs to be done yesterday already! YOU created that STRESS.

If on the other hand, you deal with work, pay the accounts, answer letters, and complete the tasks needed to be done from the INBOX each day as it comes in, then it has been processed will not still need to be done in 2 weeks time with the rest of it.

The account for instance that we were talking about earlier - by not paying anything you will get into serious trouble, finance charges etc. However if you pay as much as you can, the next time the bill comes it will be that much less, and then the person you owe money will at least see you are paying something, which is a lot better than noting is it not? They will be happy and you will be less concerned.

"Keep the INBOX clear"

Chapter 17

Naked People All Want The Same Thing!

Cars, like people are categorized, so we can identify "what" they are. Be it an Audi, Ferrari, Mercedes, Toyota or Volkswagen Beetle - they are all still "cars".

It has: an engine, wheels, a chassis, a body, doors, gearbox, seats, windows, mirrors, lights, indicators, control panels, steering wheel, seat belts and a few other items which would make it a car .... and would be found in anything called a car.

That's cars, now what about people? As with cars, people have the basics: 1 head, 2 legs, 2 arms, 10 fingers, 10 toes, 2 eyes, male or female reproductive organs, walk erect, fine body hair and torso. This would be the standard human "model", although there are exceptions as with most rules.

So where am I going with all of this you may be asking? As with cars, of the many different models and specifications, they also come from different countries. In the same way a Russian person, speaks Russian and is educated to Russian specifications. Americans, are from the United States of America, speak American English and are educated to American specifications.

This applies to each and every country, and even within those countries the region from where they originate specifies the people and so is their education and characteristics. It is these specifications that the citizens of each country and each region will base their lives and education on.

Now take these people, from all over the world, different countries, different regions, and "strip" them to the core. "Men" are men by definition, and "women" are women by definition as will "boys" be boys and "girls" are girls.

Lets imagine that all of these people are "empty" and have no form of education or experience. What is it that these individual people want, considering that they don't know about cars, houses, social standards and valuables?

When you are brought to this state, you revert to animal instinct, and survival is the focus. This means: food, water, heat, pressure, sunshine, no fighting (only survival /defending themselves), family and pleasure.

The first of this list - food, water, heat, pressure and sunshine are the most basic essential needs for any living organism to survive, but the peaceful environment, family and pleasure are essentials which are also needed, however could be lived without in extreme circumstances.

When you have absolutely nothing, and are given the choice of the basic wants and needs of life - these are those basics. To make it easier to understand, ask yourself which of the situations below you would refer to be in with regard to Peace, Love and Pleasure.

PEACE - Would you prefer to constantly be fighting with the people around you? This would include neighbors, family or the people from a distance away? Or would you rather co-habitat and enjoy the company, friendship and helpfulness as alternative?

LOVE - Do you want a partner and later a family to be with, and have some really great friends, or would you like to be lonely all your days?

PLEASURE - It is happiness, fun, enjoyment and good times, or simply being sad, silent, un-enthusiastic and bored with nothing to do?

Take your answers into mind and think of how you live on a daily basis - do you live in this way? Take this lesson and it's awareness to create the opportunities on a daily basis, which will make your life easier (and indirectly also those around you influenced by you.)

"Respect people in the way that you would like to be Respected"

Chapter 18

A Mistake Or A Lesson Opportunity

Two guys sitting in a jail cell, both having been arrested the previous evening for drunken driving, and both had car accidents as a result.

Do you know which of the two is never going to drink and drive again? Lets see, after hearing a little more about their individual car accidents. The first man, got caught running a red light, and in the process side-swiped another car and then failed to stop at the scene, but crashed into a pole down the street.

The second man also ran a red light and t-boned another car and in the process killed two children in the back seat, whilst hospitalizing the parents in the front.

Since I can remember, I was always made aware of what I was doing wrong - and when I did something and was not "told off", figured it was okay. I used to often wonder why others are so quick to let you know when you are doing something "wrong", but very slow to commend you when it is done right! At school it was simple, because teachers were quick to shout and a cane across the backside was the definite message of " WRONG DOING" or "NOT GOOD ENOUGH"!

Especially at school, time seemed to consist of doing punishment or forced to do the same work over and over again.... I can only guess that the teachers figured that a boy like myself and many like me would grasp the concept by repeatedly doing the same work making the same mistakes over and over again without further guidance??

Soon enough I realized that without "understanding" the concept, it could have been a foreign language I was being forced to repeat, and expected to learn .... especially Mathematics.

In the beginning of new work, I would try to keep up and get on with the work through understanding, which sometimes was okay.

Then on other sections - another language! To be told to do the work over and over if there was no understanding on my part, was ridiculous - so to save myself the time I would have been wasting - I focused on the subjects that I could understand and simply got caned the following day for the incomplete work, and then that was over until the next time.

There were very few teachers who seemed to understand this, and they were the only ones to sit and explain the work a different way in order to try and get the concept over.

It was actually one of these teachers who took the time to explain mathematics to me that helped me to scrape through the subject in my final year.

I learned two lessons here:
1. One must understand a concept in order to "work" with it effectively
2. Not all people in the same category are the same "character", but individuals.

My parents were more supportive and understanding of my situation, than any teacher I ever knew. Each ¼ year report displayed the results for that ¼ in each subject. At each ¼ my parents would commend me on my effort, no matter how badly the results showed because they knew that I tried my best. It was great to have that support especially when I think of some of the reports that I took home.

I have brought this up because I know that there are many teachers and parents out there who are scolding children for putting in a valiant effort, but the results may not reflect it or are not good enough...for whom? - the parent's vanity?

Some of my clients are junior school goers, and they complain to me of this still to be happening.

For parents and teachers - how about, "Good effort, but that way is a little more complex, and easier to get lost in, let me show you an easier way".

Or

"You seem to be having difficulty with the work, shall I show you another method?"

But what we do hear is, "No, that's wrong, you will do it over until you get it right, take it away I don't want to see you until you get it right".

Or

"These are your lessons - be adult about it and study it for yourself", and the   teacher goes out to do their own thing.

- How do YOU feel when you are put down and ridiculed for incompetence whilst still trying to learn the basics of something?
- How does anyone feel to be put down after a hearty effort?
- How do you feel when someone complains about the way you have done something, because it is not their way?

Is it only when we do wrong that others notice us? What has happened? Gone are the days of commending people for their effort, now it seems everyone is focused on the perfect being - "not perfect-not good enough"!

When last did you get a complement? When last did you give a compliment?

Lesson Opportunities is what this is all about. For everything that may be considered "negative", there is a positive and a lesson to be learned by looking for that "positive".

Lets go back to our example of the drunken drivers.

The first man, who clipped the side of the other car, will get license probation, slap on the wrist a fine if it is not his first offence, and be off to drive again. Give him 4 weeks of going out, not drinking and driving, and it is more than likely that he will be back to the clubs or pubs for sociable socializing including the drinks shortly after that.

The other man will probably take a few months or weeks before he even gets behind the wheel of a car again. He may also not ever touch drink again. This man has learned more than any textbook could ever show or demonstrate, through the reality of life experience.

He has also learnt:
1 - Why not to drink and drive
2 - How drinking impairs the senses
3 - What it feels like to know you destroyed an innocent family.
4 - Through personal ignorance and disrespect of the law, he took
       the lives of 2 harmless children.
5 - What it is like to live with the lives of 2 people on his
       conscience, knowing that their parents will never get to see
       their child again, is his fault.

And all of this he will live through again and again on a daily basis - pure torture. He has placed his own "Life-Sentence" on himself, never mind the jail sentence he is likely to get.

*"Take the opportunity to make the best of every situation,
and enjoy life to the full"*

Chapter 19

Attack or Withdraw

Attack or withdraw - what do you do when you are confronted by a situation that makes you feel uncomfortable? It does not mean you being in a dark alley approached by someone who you would not consider to be desirable.

It could be a simple conversation in which the person talking becomes: sexist, abusive, offensive, judgmental and critical of yourself or others, which really   presses your buttons - the wrong ones!!

Your responses could be:
To immediately respond by expressing to the individual your "opinion" which is dislike of their critical nature or manner, and by your "opinion" it does not suite the conversation, the environment, so please change the topic or stop speaking in that tone.

Attack, judge and be critical of the person yourself .... give the person a little taste of his/her own medicine! But this is NOT something I would recommend. There is however "a right time and place for everything" when the ultimate circumstance arises and the person has been the behaving in this manner for a long time and nothing has been able to help this person see the offensiveness of his/her nature.

THIS SHOULD ONLY BE DONE IF YOU YOURSELF ARE IN A POSITIVE, HEALTHY STATE OF MIND AND ARE DOING IT FOR THE BENEFIT OF THE INDIVIDUAL CONCERNED, otherwise it would simply mean that you would be lowering yourself to the level of the negative thought patterns in which the other person is stuck.

Simply get up and leave.... if it is your own home you could leave the room, or ask them to leave the house explaining that you will not tolerate "verbal or physical abuse" from anyone in your own house.

If it is not your own home and you can't leave for whatever reason, possibly the workplace, then leave the room, distance yourself from the negativity, come back after 10 minutes of having taken a breather or when the topic has changed.

If asked why you left - speak your truth: that you were offended.
Unfortunately there are many people who, when provoked, react aggressively. If you are such an individual or find yourself in this situation, get help (for yourself that is) or learn to move out of the situation whenever you feel that it is overpowering you. Get out of the situation before you do something you may regret.

By having a look at the options, you might come up with another alternative to the situation. In whatever way you look at it - your reaction when your conscious mind is discomforted by particular stimulus; a movie, a sound, a picture, a story, a thought, a dream, an opinion, a newspaper article, ... etc. - your mind will either feel good or bad, will either want to "Attack or Withdraw" in response.

It is something worth being aware of, because this could explain why certain people either: over-react or don't react at all, and how they respond to both positive and negative stimulus.

What if someone was to share with you or a group of people, an experience, which they tell you, makes them feel the most special person in the world.

What reaction would you give to this?

Some people may show appreciation and satisfaction for the happiness the individual is experiencing, whilst other people will show no joy, but respond by beginning to share (competing) and boast their own experiences thereby overriding the first person's story and leaving him/her feeling that they had a worthless experience in comparison.

These people are out there - it may even be you!! We are not always aware when we are doing something that we have always done, which may be offensive to others. One person will be sharing with others their purchase, experience, or an achievement, and in most groups there will for sure be the one person who has to be "more" or "better". This person will tell of having found a better bargain, or a greater achievement, or a far more interesting experience ... under more challenging circumstances.

They may not realize it, but they are taking away the value of another person's experience, and reliving the one they have already had.

This is "attack", and as a result the other individual will "withdraw".

When this happens too often that withdrawn person will become more and more introvert, thereby speak less and less of themselves, ultimately thinking and feeling less important.

- Do you do it?
- Do you know where you fit in?
- Do you attack or withdraw?
- Do you know why?
- Do you want it to be this way?

Read on into the next chapter to find out WHY, and how you can outgrow it.

"Be the best of being yourself, makes a better person"

Chapter 20

Who Is Pressing Your Buttons & Why?

- Are you easily affected by what other people may say or do in your company?
- Are you easily irritated or angered by what other people may be doing with them-selves around you, although it has nothing to do with you?
- Do you look at others critically - openly or to yourself?
- Do the habits of others drive you insane?

WHY? Have you any ideas as to what may be the cause of this?

From my experience, and that of others, the cause comes back to us. It is like this. If another person does something and this causes you to become emotional: love, hate, anger, frustration, irritation, pain, fear, desperation - this "trigger" will release those memories that will flood back in to your subconscious.

A memory of something you experienced earlier on in your life. It could be something that happened a day, or a week or a month or a few or even many years ago. The memory is triggered and causes you to re-experience the same emotions as you did at the time that it actually happened.

In the same way a person in a car accident may be very apprehensive of driving a car again, due to the memory of the horrific experience. A case in England where a woman was T-boned in a car crash whilst turning right, finds it impossible to turn right some years later - only turning left even if it means going 1-5 kilometers out of her way.

Similarly, someone may simply hate the fact that anyone is late, because in his previous relationship, the partner was always late and this made the individual late, so now being late causes the individual to become angry and frustrated with the person concerned.

This would be the connection on a subconscious level, but also through discomfort of arriving late, would prefer to avoid it.

The dog that has been beaten by a man or woman, and will at the sight of a raised hand or stick cringe and withdraw into itself or even be prepared to defend itself. So even if you are about to stroke the dog, the simple hand above it will trigger off the memory.

If the person who beat the dog was a man - then it is likely that the dog will only react this way when a man lifts his hand, but when a woman does it the dog may not even react.

When someone is doing something that is causing you to become emotional - think back in your life, and most of the time you will find a connection to the past!

Once this connection is found and realized, in most cases the triggering mechanism will no longer be able to trigger the emotional response of neither that memory nor the mental/physical reaction.

Your past is your past, which "you can effect as much as you can change it". The experiences through which valuable life lessons were learnt might not have been pleasant, and I would not wish your bad experience on anyone. For the sake of the present, and all those around you, take the time to ponder on the triggering mechanism, because it is not fair on the present partner or person to be suffering your wrath because of the emotional times that someone in your past caused you to experience - they are individuals, so treat them like that.

As a man, I can speak of this lesson personally. I have had a few relationships in my life and the thing that remains constant is comparison. I know that in the past I was guilty of it - so I am human after all. Comparing the character of your partner with another previous partner, and picking out qualities of a partner that you wish this partner had more of or even less of.

Some of my clients are having problems within their relationships, and once the relationship is broken up into little categories of "pro's and con's", it becomes clear that the partner is expecting from the other things that may not even have been discussed, but expect it all the same, because the previous relationship allowed those things.

Is it fair to judge on the actions of another?

Good or bad, having to pay the price for the damage or spoiling they did? Can't go to a particular place or any club, because your partner's ex-partner spent their life in the club?

Don't go out to dinner because the partner's ex-partner was always dragging them out to functions and hotels for parties?

Can't touch a partner lovingly and with fun because the ex used to start off that way and become abusive or rough? And so on.

What do you deny your partner because it is something your ex-partner used to do which you disliked then, so won't do it now - is that fair?

Keep this in mind because if someone else is doing something that you allow yourself to become emotional about, remember that it is a past memory being triggered, which you should try to disconnect from. Try and figure out why or who did that to bug you back then, understand this and it will no longer have the effect on you when a different person does it.

"You can effect your past as much as you can change it"

Chapter 21

I Would If..., I Should...But...

How often do you find yourself saying the word..."I should" ... or... " I could" in typical conversation in a day? Once, twice, three or more times a day? Then there is always a reason, which follows the "I should" with a BUT, or IF.

"I should take a holiday, BUT I simply can't find the time" or "I could go on holiday, IF I could find the time"

It is a part of everyday life, "I should fix the tap but ... ", "I would go to town if..."

As life and time has gone by, we have become "Couch Potatoes", almost too lazy to do anything that can't be done over the phone, Internet or by remote control, especially if it is not pre-planned. Thinking that if the house is not falling down, the tap's leak is not flooding the house, then "it" can be done tomorrow or the next day, "if I have time"..............

Write down 5 things that you know you SHOULD do:

      I should...
      I should...
      I should...
      I should...
      I should...

Now write 5 things that you know you WOULD like to do:
      I would...
      I would...
      I would...
      I would...
      I would...

Read all 10 sentences back to yourself aloud. Are these things really out of reach? What are your excuses for not doing what you know you SHOULD do, and for what you WOULD do? Are these excuses valid or just a way out from doing it?

To complete this exercise, answer all 10 sentences by replacing SHOULD or WOULD with COULD.

Example 1

I SHOULD walk the dog today, but don't have any extra time.

Becomes: I COULD walk the dog today if I made some extra time by getting up a half hour earlier.

Example 2

I WOULD be more supportive of others if they were supporting me

Becomes: I COULD become more supportive of others by looking to myself for support rather than others.

Now do those 10 sentences with COULD. Once you have completed those sentences, re-read them aloud to yourself.

For a last confirmation that it COULD be done, replace the COULD with CAN in each sentence, to make it really inspiringly positive. And use it as your affirmation!

My philosophy is *"WHAT'S DONE IS DONE"*

Chapter 22

The Bumble Bee

The Bumble Bee is a humble creature,
It goes about doing it's own thing not bothering anyone
It weighs only 2 grams, and has a wing surface area of 2cm squared
According to the laws of physics
With these dimensions it should be impossible to fly
But - the bumblebee knows of no such limits
And continues to fly doing it's own thing.

The power of choice and the power of the mind come into play here. Think about people bending objects with their minds, levitating, practically stopping their breath over long periods of time, and all these fantastic feats that have been displayed to us over the years. You can do those or something special too!

The Bumblebee goes about deciding what to do when and where, and how it wants to. It does not have a painful family member saying what it should or should not be doing, or how to do it.

We too are as individual as the Bumblebee, and have the power to choose which flower we go to or how high to fly, how far we are prepared to go or not go.

As the Bumble bee, knows no limits, only set your own standards on a flexible cord, so they can be changed whenever YOU feel that they need to alter.

Remove the LIMITS and begin to access the POWER within.
The book is about removing these limits and boundaries from your life – use the information where you can to make life that bit easier and stress-free.

ANTHONY LYLE SMITH

"Be spontaneous, be free, be your own Bumble Bee."

Chapter 23

Process

A Process is -i.e. path of events that FOLLOW: Everything in life has a process.... it could be a plant starting in the form of a seed, growing into a plant, flowering and then dying after spreading it's seeds for new plants to grow in its place.

The human being - is reproduced by being conceived, develops, grows, matures, mates and then dies after leaving behind an offspring that will follow that same path and process, just as the flower did, whilst the body is returned to the earth where it will fertilize plants growing organisms.

The process may be short or it may be long, depending upon what it is. So far we have been talking about how your life is affected by these "things", and of ways of understanding why or how they work. Your life and the processes within it; on a physical, mental, spiritual and emotional level - all have begun somewhere and will end somewhere, once stability has been regained or the process itself has come to an end.

To make this more obvious, take the Digestive System. It has a process that involves (very basic description): the intake of food, the breakdown of that food into the most simple form, the absorption of that broken down food, and then the elimination of the remains, known as waste. (Which could and should be used to fertilize crops being grown)

You control what goes in, and more or less when the waste leaves. You certainly cannot go and sit in the toilet having a mighty "shit", and then decide half way through that, this is enough and the process is over because you don't want to do that anymore.

It would be understandable if a bomb went off, but under normal circumstances to try and stop this part of the digestive process could be harmful not to mention uncomfortable as time goes on.

When you start a relationship, which involves physicality and emotion, the relationship will either continue beyond the grave, or will end when the emotions and physical relationship cease to exist.

Relationships are the quickest process we start and the hardest to stop or end due to the mental and emotional ties that we store in our minds and hearts, and this means that only thinking of someone can bring back those emotional ties.

"If you can change it –then there is no need to worry,
And if you can't change it - then what's the point in worrying"

Settle the process to the point that it's officially over and done with - be honest about that. If you have an ounce of doubt that the process is not over then it is not, and will bother you on a sub-conscious level until it is over.

If something is bothering you, then look to the process in which it is, and ask yourself if it is finished or not. Then you will know if you still have work on it to finish or not.

" If it is in your cycle - keep processing it"

Chapter 24

A Rose Amongst The Thorns

- Does your environment influence your life-style?
- Does your environment influence your ways... choices and alternatives to do things a way that would not be your first option?

If it does, it really should not. Nature provides us with the perfect example of this in the Lotus Flower. The Lotus Flower is one of the most beautiful flowers yet it is found growing in some of the most unsuitable environments and water. The "state" of it's environment does not influence the flower, and prevent it from living it's own life and flowering into the beautiful flower it truly is.

The Lotus Flower plant takes from the muddy and polluted waters, only the particles it needs, and does not allow the waste elements into the system.

You too can live your life as a Lotus Flower being sure to only take from your environment that which will suit your needs and prevent the rest from getting in.

Sure you may live in a bad environment, and things can of course get rough, but are you going to allow other people to affect how you choose to grow and mature, to become who they want you to be or to become who you would like to be?

In the same way as the Lotus Flower makes it's choice of which elements may enter and become a part of it's life, to ensure it becomes the best it possibly can, you too can choose your elements (people / influences) and only allow in those parts that will allow your personal growth and development in the positive that way you want.

.Yes, people may laugh, call you names or judge you for standing up for yourself, but it "takes a lot more courage to change than it does to stay the same" and do what everyone else wants you to do. If you change - it means that they could change too, and this alone would scare many people.

Once again nature provides us with a prime example - sheep. It is well known that sheep follow one another everywhere.

So, if one sheep goes over a wall or through to the next field where there is less or very little grass - nearly all the other sheep will follow and in doing so leave behind a field with rich and luscious grass only because the first one went over the fence.

Occasionally you will find a small group of sheep on their own, perhaps like the ones that did not go over the wall, which seem to have made up their own minds to stay where things suited them better.

The choice is in your hands: either "follow the leader" like sheep to bare pastures, or "be the leader" by living life by the example of the Lotus Flower, taking from your environment what you need.

"The well trodden path means it is well used, but does not mean that it goes your way"

Chapter 25

Leading By Experience

... Because talk is cheap. Anyone can tell another person how to do something, or what they should be doing, but where is that knowledge coming from?

Think of driving a car. An experienced driver giving a novice directions just sitting beside him without previous demonstration, could be something like this: put the clutch in, put first gear into place, push the gas pedal down and now simultaneously let the clutch out and you're driving - repeat the process to change gears.

Easier said than done. Directions like this from my eldest sister turned my fathers car into a Kangaroo within seconds of me getting behind the wheel.

However, the above instructions were then demonstrated with a verbal commentary, the concept was made easier and I then understood it.

Only give advice or "instructions" once you have the experience to do so, but not if you do not feel sure, or worse if you have never personally experienced it.

Another simple but common example:

The engagement ring is something that many women in a long term relationship may begin to "wish for" at some stage -"ooh, is that ring not nice?" " Susan got such a beautiful diamond ring from John, did you see?" And other more or less subtle hints

Remember in such cases, that diamonds are not cheap. Acknowledge that it may not be affordable to your partner! Remind yourself that the price today to be paid for, for a diamond ring might just cost your partner everything in finance and mental energy that they have!!

Have you ever bought yourself a ring of this price for yourself?

The reason for this example is quite simple: LEAD BY EXAMPLE AND EXPERIENCE. Do you know, and are you aware of sacrifices that may have to be made to afford such a ring? Not everyone can pay cash for diamonds these days. Could you make that commitment (to) yourself?

Once you have done this for yourself, and you know that your partner can make and would commit him to that "gift" -then by all means go ahead and hint away.

But, it is important to be aware of the situation and emotional distress that you are putting your partner in, bear in mind when he / she is asked something like this and doesn't have the "resources" or the ability to such a commitment - how does it make him / her feel: wanting desperately to satisfy your "needs" or "wants", but not being able to afford it?

A ring is a simple example, common enough among people today in relationships, but it might not be the ring, it could be anything from jewellery to furniture, clothes, a car, and a house..... We all come from different levels of the food chain and wealth on the planet, so if you are the one carrying wads of cash in your pocket, consider what your remarks might do to the one without it.

The "price" of the item being asked may not be in Punts, Dollars, or Francs but in the person's: time, commitment, sacrifice, emotions, mental and physical energy, which can also be very expensive.

So, when asking something of another person - be sure that they can afford the "price". It might well not be a diamond ring, but perhaps a new car, house, piece of equipment, tools, new decorations or something as simple as a new carpet in the house.

You will know this by having experienced this yourself, and by getting to know the person you are asking a bit first, so you know their financial and "energy" reserves and their capabilities.

"By doing it yourself - you now what it takes to get it done"

Chapter 26

Expectation

"If you don't expecting anything from anyone -
You won't feel hurt when you get nothing
Expect too much - you will never appreciate a little"

This is about enjoying your own company, and what you can provide for yourself. If you are happy with yourself, then others will be happy with you - it will be shared. And if you are not happy with yourself and can't enjoy your own company - you cannot expect others to share in your misery and unhappiness too - they won't.

When you do something for yourself, enjoy it. When you are doing something for someone else - do it because you want to - enjoy doing that too, otherwise don't - do not do it at all, if it is going to cause you that much discomfort.

Do for others when you want to because you want to, and don't be expecting them to reward you back with a favor... or you will begrudge them if they don't offer you one in return.

In situations where you are not getting paid for what you are doing because it is not your job, you need to make sure that when you do it - that it is unconditional. Unconditional means that you will not be expecting anything back in return - you did it because you were asked, and were able to at the time.

Doing something on a conditional basis, will only ensure hurt and disappointment when the "reward" is not available or there is none on offer afterwards. Don't expect anything, and you will feel great to have been able to help Expect something and you will be disappointed when you get nothing

"Life's little rewards come when you least expect them"

Chapter 27

The Fisherman & The Wealthy Businessman

A day in a quiet place, a fisherman sat on the end of pier fishing.
A well-dressed man approached him, and began speaking to him.

"Say, why is it that you are sitting here in the middle of the day fishing?"

"Can you not you see that I am not only sitting, but I am fishing - what should I be doing?"

"Well you could be working for one thing ", said the man

"Why should I be working?" asked the fisherman

" If you work, you can earn lots of money", replied the man

"Then what am I to do with lots of money? ", questioned the fisherman.

"With lots of money you can buy a small business which can work for you", exclaimed the rich man

"And what do I do when I have a small business working for me, making lots of money?" asked the fisherman.

"Then you can afford the luxuries of life -cars, boats, yachts, houses and holidays whenever you wish", answered the rich man.

"But what If I don't want any of those expensive, luxurious things?" asked the fisherman

"Then, my friend you can do whatever it is you wish to do with your time and money," Said the rich man and the fisherman replied,

"So then why did you ask me why I was sitting here fishing on the pier - when I am doing with my time and money what I want to - I don't have all your luxuries, and I don't need them- I am happy with my life just the way it is?"

So here you see it, life through two peoples eyes. Some people need the money to have the comfort and life's pleasures, whilst others don't need more than the simple pleasures of life to keep them content.

You decide what you need - it's not about "keeping up with the Jones's", but keeping yourself happy at the end of the day.

"There are two sides to every story – don't be quick to decide"

Chapter 28

More Is Not Always Better?

Having more of something than a fair helping can make you sick ....
food can poison you, alcohol - intoxicates you, and if it is mismanaged
wealth, it can make for a really complicated life.

Think of a family in India - a normal family, nothing special, 8-10 people
living under one roof, grand-parents, parents, children, uncles and aunts,
and possibly only one income for all of them to survive on. Some
families are lucky enough to earn the equivalent of $10 per month on
which they must all survive, cloth and feed as well as maintain and
educate the family members. The hard to believe fact is reality, and a
common one at that.

As little as they may have, life is about survival - not the latest car, new
Nintendo games and designer underwear. For them it's making it
through each day with a full belly, and a little to cover the expenses like
basic clothing, food and education costs which are high when you are
earning $10 a month. The people don't "have to have" a cell phone, a
disc-man, a DVD player, a car for each family member, designer clothes,
stereo systems, TV, video, and disco every other night, insurance,
medical plans, car insurance, house insurance, life insurance, assortment
of crockery, wardrobes full of clothes, full of shoes, holidays in the
mountains, swimming pool and all the other bits and pieces of modern
day society.

Compare this - with someone living in one of those posh suburbs of any
of our cities, and think of all the commitments they have to make each
day before feeding a max of 3 or 4? The cleaner, the garden service, the
pool-boy, the maid, the secretary, the chauffeur, the security company,
medical plan, life insurance, school fees, college fund, cars for everyone
over 16 in the family, sports equipment, country club, overseas holidays,
cosmetic surgery, top of the line cars... and much more of even basic

necessities like: clothes, shoes, stereo systems, CD players, DVD players, MP3 players, computers and everything in your home had to be paid for.

In modern society luxury comes first.

Take a look around your room at home, or work and list 20 different items, and the function that each of those items has in your life.

1. ....
2. ....
3. ....
4. ....
5. ....
6. ....
7. ....
8. ....
9. ....
10. ....
11. ....
12. ....
13. ....
14. ....
15. ....
16. ....
17. ....
18. ....
19. ....
20. ....

Look at that list again and think of all those things you could do without and the true value of them in terms of survival on a daily basis?

Are they society survival aides (necessities) or just luxuries?

Sometimes we need a wake up call, which will show us just exactly what it is we have. When we don't have it, we suddenly realize that it is a luxury and we actually could survive quite easily without it. A good example of this would be the cell phone, which up until a few years ago this gadget did not exist, and we all survived just fine. I am aware that they have a place in "modern- day living" which makes life that much easier, but at the same time, look how lazy we have become as a result, and the normal life is gone. People survived very well without the cell phone, before that they also got on very well without the telephone, - but we are not realizing that the more modern technology comes into play in our lives the more of ourselves we are losing.

If you have forgotten what it feels like to be "normal", try going a day without some sort of "luxury" like a cell-phone, electricity, a computer, an electric stove, or the radio and television, yes even without your car.

For a day you will get a taste of reality, and for longer than that you will get to feel reality, and will have to use your brain to entertain yourself for a change.

As a gift to yourself, take one day a week e.g. Sunday, and go without all the technology that is ruling your life, and make that day yours, come back to Earth, root level, for a few hours and find yourself to make contact again.

"You did not need it before it was invented, so why let your life depend on it now?"

Chapter 29

Diet

There is a wonderful myth about dieting which I would like to discuss, and hopefully through the information there will be some people, which shall benefit as a result.

The information is for people, who are relatively healthy, and weight is their only "problem", otherwise there may be things like hormonal imbalance, thyroid imbalance, stress fear etc, which we will not go into at this stage.

The dieting I am going to talk about is not about: bathroom scales, calories, and today's weight compared to last weeks weight, or yesterdays weight, and then again it is everything that I am going to talk about. Diet is about the way you combine your foods, and the way you supply your body with the essentials that it needs to keep you healthy.

It is important to remember that the suggestions and information I am giving you are my opinion, and any views which I have, does not to mean that what your nutritionist or doctor or specialist may have told you is wrong. Consult your particular specialist if you decide to take the information, before you begin to use it.

As far as I am concerned, due to us all being individuals that differ in DNA, cell level (which determines who, how, what we are) our diets should be just as individually approached.

In the same way as one person may advise me to listen to Mozart when I am feeling tense because that is what relaxes this particular person, I may find Mozart most disturbing when I am feeling tense, however the sound of Dolphins and water might do the trick for me.

118

What works for one person, does not mean it will work for the next, you will be lucky if 10 out of every 100 have the same first choice when stressed. Always bear this in mind when dieting.

Are you lucky enough to be able to eat whatever you like in whatever portions you like without putting on any weight, and without having to do any exercise?

If yes, count yourself lucky for now, and take in the following information for when the day might come when that changes.

If on the other hand you are not so lucky to be able to eat whatever, whenever and however much you choose - are you the person who looks at a slice of bread and puts on weight?

This could possibly be explained to you in many different scientific ways, but that is not what I am about to do. I have my own explanations about weight loss and weight gain.

The first is about INHERITANCE, in the form of genes - not Levi's. These are characteristic traits that come from your bloodline, or ancestry - your parents, their parents, and theirs, and so on. Genes are an every-person thing, whether you like it or not you are wearing these ones.

The sad thing, is that many people only recognize the "dis-eased" genes like: Cancer, Alzheimer's, Arthritis, etc.... etc, after it has manifested itself as such. Most people have those diseased genes within them, however the "right environment" (internal body state, as with plants in the right soil) must be in place before the seed can grow.

For example Arthritis -: with a lot of self-love, and looking after yourself already in from early years, can prevent Arthritis from "establishing".
Avoid acid forming foods and maintain a high Calcium, Magnesium, Vitamin D levels, as well as a constant high level of vitamins and minerals.

- Do you feel that your life is sad?
- Are you feeling depressed?
- Stuck in the vicious circle?
- Not able to do much because you are also not trying hard enough to get out of it?

Plus - is your food made up of the junk food category loaded with artificial enhancer and preservatives (mostly acid producing), and definitely not natural, which means not good nutrition for the body.

CONGRATULATIONS - You, yourself have provided yourself with the "environment" in which arthritis thrives.

I can hear you ask -"How do I get out of such a situation, or know where my weaknesses lie?"

As an Iridologist myself, I would suggest to visit an Iridologist. Iridology is the study of the iris of the eyes, and through the markings found on the Iris and around the eye, the Iridologist can determine the condition of the tissues of the different organs and body systems, and will be able to tell you where your body needs help and how you can go about helping it through diets avoiding e.g. acid forming foods.

The Iris reflects high levels of acid in the system, which is the acute or the beginning sign of complications, which your body is unable to get rid of or neutralize by itself.

This body weakness may be either inherited or something considered a "life-style" attributed factor.

Smoking is another simple example, where the Iridologist can quite easily see Lung tissue weakness marking which are usually visible by the naked eye. The information given to you would be: suggestion to stop smoking, and herbal or homeopathic lung support remedies to assist the body in the repair and strengthening of that tissue.

So, Iridology would be one way to find out where you need to watch your body, by simply knowing which organs are already "weaker" than others.

The other way which is not as diagnostic as Iridology, but works just as well.

Everything in moderation... yes exactly that. Many people know that they eat or drink too much.

Meat is for carnivores, and we are primates, so if you must eat meat make sure that you are not placing your body under excess strain by eating it every day but maximum 1- 2 times a week, then making sure that you only choose very lean beef, veal or poultry (no pork, as pork has very long processing time through your digestive system).

Fish, preferably Salmon or Mackerel is better for you and much easier on the body with its Omega3 oils, 2-3 times per week.

Vegetables should be eaten with every meal (except breakfast), unless you are eating a fruit meal. Lots of green leafy vegetables, which to take care not to over cook, so as they don't lose all their nutritional value. Mixed salads with freshly picked garden herbs should be also eaten once a day to help balance the diet.

Fruit can and should be eaten daily, making the perfect snack meal, or the perfect craving buster for those trying to give up smoking.

The plant or vegetable based diet is healthiest, although some research is "proving" that chocolate can be good for the heart and meat is also good for the system.

I just wonder how good the heart does after all that chocolate, and the teeth, and the immune system and the blood sugar levels ... and the other body systems that have to clean up after it!!

Gorillas are the largest of the primate family of which we are members, and are unmatched in strength, and yet live on a plant, leaf, fruit and root based diet? How can we say that we cannot only eat that food, and that it is not enough?

Elephants are not primates, and neither is the Rhinoceros' - but look at their size and strength, and they live off leaves, grasses, fruits and berries.

Yes, I do realize that we are not living in trees and we don't hang out in the communal cave on the weekend, and I am not suggesting that you to go off and eat leaves, berries and grasses. But, what I am reminding you of, is that we don't "need" all this stuff that we think we do in order to survive.

Try to eat in moderation - which means: when I don't eat, I get hungry - then I eat- and when I do eat, I eat until I am satisfied not stuffed and won't eat until the next hunger. If you get hungry in between main meals –get yourself a piece, or even a couple of pieces of fruit.

This is my basic diet: plant based, with the occasional piece of meat, or fish, or poultry, once in while a piece of chocolate, once in a while a glass of beer, or organic wine, and, yes, the odd piece of pizza.

After all I have told you, you may be wondering why this diet. The answer to this is: "Everything In Moderation". Now, with this in mind, I may only have a steak once in 4-5 months, and beer 1 bottle in a 10 days, chocolate one small bar in 20 days, wine I'd have more often say one bottle emptied over the course of a fortnight, and pizza say every three months. Every other day it's potatoes, rice, corn, maize, or soy, and fish about twice a week, poultry once a fortnight and all meals always accompanied by vegetables or salads. Now, how bad does that diet seem now?

You see junk foods are exactly that - junk, and there is very little that our bodies can do with the by-products. However, in most generations unless you are more "mature" and wise, you would have been brought up on sweets, chocolates, biscuits, artificial foods and the rest of the junk out there, which means that for many people a chocolate is just as important in the shopping basket as the apples.

It is the more healthy foods that people put last into the basket. I am aware of some people who only know how to prepare microwave foods, and so that is all they eat. It is not their fault - it is what they grew up knowing.

Now, as with alcoholics, drug addicts, caffeine addicts or chocoholics or anyone with an addictive habit -the nature of the sickness is the ADDICTION, and it is this disease of addiction that drives our bodies to become dependant on certain substances: be it alcohol, marijuana, cocaine, caffeine, sugar or nicotine. These products have become something used by you for the body on a daily basis to "support" your needs, and your body has become dependant, or addicted on certain "junk" foods for your daily "fix", which is the driving force behind continuous use.

But, if we were to stay off some of these products for a while, you will feel the body starting to become more balanced and less demanding of the product/s (junk), and when you do crave the chocolate or whatever it may be: have it and enjoy it in a small dose, and that will satisfy the craving.

Or on the other hand commit yourself to not having any of it anymore then and there and stand your ground. I am not referring to the drugs or alcohol any more, those would be best left alone completely at once. But food that you crave: fight the craving, But if the craving just won't go away you will fight the energy right out of yourself, and the stress of trying not to have that chocolate or whatever it may be will cause your body more harm than the small piece of chocolate would.

By fighting the craving, in one way, you are showing yourself you can resist, which is excellent! On the other hand it is okay to give in at the beginning because the stress will keep your mind focused on chocolate, and until you have a piece it will stay focused on it, until you satisfy your body's need.

CRAVING 1	CRAVING 2
• Craving chocolate • Buy smallest one and eat it. • Craving satisfied • Okay	• Craving chocolate • How to avoid raving eat fruit -still craving = mind remains on craving • Distracted • Try feeling good for not giving in • Craving • Dying and body crying intense craving • Still holding on • Really stressed • Buy large slab - Over-indulge Feel sick had too much • Craving satisfied • Now okay.

Cravings are important to look at, because they will actually tell you what your body is really looking for:

· Potassium you can get from a banana
· Sugar, you can get from an apple
· Calcium, you can get from milk

Listen to your body, do some research and give it what it craves in a nutritional way.

Chapter 30

The Not Eating Properly, or Too Little Diet

What were spoken about in the last chapter were two approaches of "dieting". Another method of dieting for many people is to "NOT EAT" which they believe will cause them to carry less, because they are putting less in.

In my opinion this "not eating" works in two ways.

1. It causes all fat and every other little bit excess matter around the body to be absorbed by the body to provide the energy and building equipment to maintain the body, which leaves people very thin or anorexic.

2. Safety Mode - Who are these people and who does it effect? The people tend to be obese, or fat. Men and women, boys and girls - who either eat too much, or eat the wrong foods, or eat combining the wrong food groups.

In many cases diagnosed through blood tests, it is found to be either hormonal or thyroid malfunctioning. But in many cases these people are told to look at their diets and lifestyles because the tests show nothing "abnormal". The majority of obese people are found to be medically sound.

Have you heard of the saying "You are what you eat"? I don't ever recall hearing someone say, "You are what you don't eat".

If you were to eat 3 square meals a day, you would be healthy and not overweight. However if you were to eat 3 junk meals a day, you would be overweight and possibly a sickly person.

For the people who are trying to loose weight by eating only one meal a day.... why is it that they put on more weight when eating less, and others eating three meals a day shed the weight?

To demonstrate the concept, I return to nature's examples:

How will a tree grow if it is kept well nourished by water and minerals from the soil and warmed by the sunlight?

Without a doubt, it is going to grow into a healthy tree.

What about a tree that is in a very hard soil, in the shade and does not get enough water and minerals from the soil - it is quite obvious that the tree will not do very well.

So, why should people be any different? If you give your body the water, sunlight, food, and minerals that it needs to function effectively and efficiently, it too will grow well and stay healthy as the well-nourished tree.

A person not giving the body enough water, sunlight, minerals and food and nourishment will notice the malfunctioning, the loss of energy pretty soon.

- Good nourishment means good leaves or building blocks
- Poor nourishment means poor quality building material, and weaker organs or leaves.
- Good nourishment means health and function (including the 5 basic elements of life).
- Poor nourishment means poor health and malfunction, loss of energy and sickness.

If that was not a little inspiration to get you thinking a little differently about food, then I shall show you the more scientific approach.

The more detailed approach requires a little more explanation, so here it is. You first need to understand a little about the digestive system, in order to understand quicker.

When you chew food you break it down the saliva already starts the digestive process, then it goes into your stomach where the acid begins to break it down a little more, then it travels on to the duodenum where the stomach acid is neutralized by bile from the gall bladder, and the pancreas provides the digestive enzymes to break down hardier particles with the assistance of the sugar balance. It then moves on to the small intestines where moisture, vitamins and minerals are removed, on to the large colon, which shapes the stools and again withdraws vitamins and moisture back in to the system.

Through this system, there are different receptors, which are there to absorb different particles, each receptor has target particles that it will absorb, and other receptors will have other target particles from the digestive process. These receptors are like little fingers, which clamp onto the particle, and then draw the particle into itself to "eat" it, from where the "energy" will be sent to wherever in the body it is needed. Amongst these receptors are also FAT receptors, which as the others absorb the above-mentioned particles, absorb fat.

When your life is normal and there is nothing bothering you, the body senses this and will function at a normal "rate". There is nothing causing you to be hasty about things, or cause your body to "stress". This means that the particles passing those receptors will pass through at a comfortable rate where the receptors have time to pick and choose the right particles and allow, that which is not needed to pass through as waste.

However, when one is under "stress" and the body systems are forced to work faster, everything down to the last cell within your body will work faster. This means that the particles will also pass through the digestive system faster... this is what is often referred to as a runny stomach (diahorrea).

What happens now is that the body still needs food and energy, so what it does to make sure that it gets enough is, it focuses on the biggest particles which are fat particles, and stores them for later. FAT particles can be broken down and used by the body for just about everything -so it is convenient. This is what I call SAFETY MODE. The body needs to take drastic measures in order to be sure that it has the resources for building blocks and repair, so begins to absorb and store those FAT particles in the buttocks, thighs and hips.

Not only does stress cause the absorption of fat, but also poor diet. You see, fat can be used for many different things when it is broken up, but the body also needs other vitamins and minerals that help it break down that fat faster, and without those the process takes longer. A plant-based diet will provide the tools for this job.

The SAFETY MODE is when the body begins to store, as it says to itself and its other parts; "We don't know when we will get the next normal supply of food and nourishment take what you can and store it for later" The body by having reserves is only thinking of survival, and by storing fat it thinks it is safe.

A bushman has a big rump - do you now know why?

The SAFETY MODE is why, and it is to ensure he always has a form of energy, even when he is stuck out in the desert with no form of nourishment.

A bushman has a big bum, for the same reason that a camel has a hump - storage. Both the bushman and the camel have two things in common - the both live in an extreme environment and there is no such thing as a square balanced diet.

Traveling through the desert as they both do, they are not sure of the next stop for food or drink, so the body takes this into consideration, and stores fat for the body to burn off as fuel whilst there is no food available. This is what I call the SAFETY MODE, and it is as common to you and me as it is to the camel and the bushman.

The SAFETY MODE is an internal mechanism by the body to ensure that you never go without fuel to keep the body driving. When you eat a well balanced diet consisting of a minimum of 3 main meals a day plus fruit, plenty of water and exercise, the SAFETY MODE will remain idle, but as soon as you stop giving your body any one of those items, it becomes ACTIVE, and then begins to store fuel reserves because you are denying it what it is used to or what it needs.

The SAFETY MODE triggered off by junk food, stress and a poor diet. As soon as your body does not get a few regular meals in after the other it switches to begin storing. So, to prevent this from happening, or from continuing - you have got to convince the body that it no longer needs to store.

This is not going to happen overnight, you are going to have to really spoil the body with only the best to "bribe" it, to stop storing and start using the good stuff! The meals have to be at least 3 times a day, and include all the elements of a good balanced diet, but those of the fruit vegetable and roots, nuts and seeds, first and foremost.

Once it starts using the nourishment, it will start burning up and allowing the fat to leave the body, also with the assistance of the new tools and equipment built by the nourishment.

Those people who simply just eat one meal a day, and still put on weight? Would you not also consider this stress?

Think of the tree, without nourishment:
1. It is being undernourished, and does not know when and if it is going to get more food energy.
2. In the day at least two meals of nutrition are missing and it needs to get this from somewhere - if it does not get it from you.

As with the other forms of stress, the body goes into safety mode, and stores EVERYTHING it can, rather than eliminate it, so store to convert it to energy later. Although you may be only eating one meal a day and still going to the toilet to eliminate waste once a day, it is the waste of the body working with what it has will make the system work and move on as best it can.

The moral of dieting is:

"EAT HEALTHY FOOD AS OFTEN AS YOU NEED IT".

It is important to remember that unless you have an imbalance in the hormones or some other area of your system, you can eat as much healthy food as you like, and will not put on weight, only that to suite your frame.

STRESS, JUNK FOOD AND IRREGULAR EATING HABITS INDUCE THE SAFETY MODE

Chapter 31

Culture And Tradition Vs Y2K

Culture and tradition have been apart of mans life for centuries. I bet it would even go back as far as the cave man. He makes a kill and drags it back to the cave, where the women makes the fire, skins and prepares the animal to be used for food, tools, clothing and warmth.

This could be seen as both culture and tradition. The culture was such that men foraged and hunted while the women tended to the "stone palace": polished and swept, cooked and clothed the family. The tradition of it is that is how life was - man hunted while the woman mothered.

Coming forward a couple of thousand years to the year 2001, much has changed ... and very little has changed. There are many families today where the man alone is the provider, and the woman "makes home" ... is it Culture or Tradition! This all depends on if you consider yourself a caveman or cave-woman or not at all.

When you think about it, Culture and Tradition are two of the same. Culture is a more "refined" way of saying the manner or approach to life by a particular group, community, countries citizens or religious group.

Tradition is basically the way this particular community, countries citizens, or religious sect have done one or more things over time in a pattern or methodical manner.

So really, the "refined" say that they will keep to traditional ways and traditional people say, lets keep to the ways of our culture as it has always been.

Now that we know the "difference", we can look into the topic on a slightly deeper level.

I am sure you know the culture or tradition by which you live as an individual .... but are you happy?

Are you happy with the way in which you are meant to fit into it, or the way in which it sets your limits and boundaries? Does it mould and set guidelines by which you must adhere to (in order not to be shunned by others) within that environment?

Does it support your choices as an individual, or does it condemn personal opinion?

This may seem a little harsh, but when one has been in such a "culture" for so long, one seems to forget ones own needs, wants and desires in order to keep within the boundaries as set by tradition of that Culture. In the chapter I would ... I Should, you will be able to see how much of your time is dedicated to this cause and that of others.

In today's modern society of the year 2002, we have indeed moved on from Cave-man to Techno-Man. Today's life is filled with the demands of society; clothes, car, house, money, appliances, computers, insurance, cell phones and the latest technology - all to make life "easier". The naturalness of life has gone, and we have adapted our lives into the technology, computers, electronic devices and nearly everything in your daily life, unless you are living in a tree in the jungle, without anything electrical or not hand-made.

Think about it - any computer, other than perhaps a mainframe system will be running on a Windows 3.1, 95, 98, 99 or 2000,Me Edition, based system. It is something that has made life that much easier, where most programmes are designed to do most of the work for you, and all other programmes run from or within that - your Windows network on your desk, to someone else's computer in the tree in the jungle, to the snowy Antarctica, or to the depths of Northern Russia and the deserts of North Africa - and lets not forget our latest frontier -SPACE ... it's so daily now that reports on space missions and travel are basically "normal".

And that is life - by no choice of your own you are living it, and by culture or tradition will determine how you live it - or out of personal choice live it the best way that you can.

Please don't turn your back on your heritage, because that is who you are, but always put your survival needs first.

It is a sad scenario really, but whether you like it or not the planet is being continually developed and destroyed by modern technological developments, where one developer believes they are doing good work, whilst the other is noticing the destruction going on and trying to make his/her business on the planet work with the planet rather than against it. For many people, the belief is to save what we have we need to change what we have?

This means to save a culture you need to completely change it ...... and then once it is all gone. This "good" work (rain forests being cut down and seas polluted with oil / toxic chemicals)... This they call modernization and progress for which we are all responsible.

If you keep up with developments as most home-owners, you are likely to feel comfortable enough not to feel left behind, and if you decide not to buy into the technology, then good on you - everyone needs to take responsibility for their for their decisions and be able to accept the consequences as a result.

When life offers you the opportunity to "stay out of it all" like the Eskimo's, Indians of the forests and Nepalese Nomads - lucky you! Sure we are all affected in one way or another -i.e. Eskimos driving snowmobiles and having to work from the oil companies that have taken over and ruined their land, but the majority of life for most is natural.

"Life is about choices - make your own"

Chapter 32

Boundary's & Limits

Unless you are not breaking the law, and are not causing yourself, an animal or any one else any harm.... the sky is the marker beacon to which you should aim, once there you can set yourself another marker.

Everyone knows the age old saying of "The sky is the limit", well from what has happened in the last 20 odd years, man has been to space, beyond the sky many times already which just proves that the sky is most definitely NOT the limit. If you want you can for the next 10 years say that Mars is the limit, as this is as far as they have sent anything -so far.

In life, yes, we should have "boundaries and limits" in connection with what we do and how we live to keep us at our own standards, but CIRCUMSTANTIAL boundaries and limits are the key. The reason for this is that a boundary or a limit is a set point or level to which you or something is set, and beyond which you or something may not or cannot go.

The limit in a small aeroplane without special pressurization equipment would be 10 000 feet simply because the PILOT has air restriction, as well as the aeroplane having difficulty staying aloft in the thin air.

A box with fixed boundaries or sides is understandable, where only so much can be contained within that space.

But coming back to you. You are the focus here, and your boundaries are questionable. What boundaries and limits do you place upon yourself and your life? How often do you say or think of the words, "I can't, or "I won't"? What about "I should not"… why not?

Do you know that every time that you tell yourself that you "should not" or "can't" it is a programme by which your brain reacts, and will be convinced that you can't or shouldn't. The brains response to this stimulus would be to remind you with an uncomfortable feeling about doing those things that you should not or cannot do, so you actually start to believe yourself that this is your truth.

Before you learnt to drive, it would have been either," I cannot drive", or "I have not learnt to drive yet", so what is the difference with other things in life that you have not taken the time to learn? Not doing because you have not experienced or tried it, does not mean that you cannot do or accomplish, does it?

Why is it, that when there is something that we want to do in the future, we will make up a reasonable explanation as to why we have not done it up to this point.

Then when it is something that we are unsure or feel uncomfortable with, we begin to make excuses, simply because we have not been exposed to it yet, for example: "I don't understand how or why", or "I cant", or "If only", we automatically become defensive. Have you ever tried it?

Now on the other hand we tend to set boundaries of thought.

Example:
One man sees what he believes to be a UFO. The friend does not believe in UFO's and has not seen one himself, so sets a mind boundary that " I have not seen therefore I do not believe"

Are you like this, because if you are you can still change -I did. Think about it, nobody has seen the Easter bunny or Father Christmas, and yet "everyone" celebrates it, gets dressed up, buys tons of goodies, has a festival, buys a tree but has anyone actually seen him flying across the evening sky at night in a sled behind Reindeer?

We live life like this to celebrate things we cannot know exist, even spend money on its account but we have not seen. I think it is great. Live for the sake of living! So why can we not take a UFO for instance in the same light and celebrate or "believe" if you have not seen it either?

About 10 years ago, I too was in this place where I would not believe anything, unless I could physical see or touch whatever it was, or someone could provide me with enough evidence to satisfy me.........

I should have applied to the FBI. I suddenly realized how ignorant I was being. It actually all began with a friend of mine, Andrew who had snakes and other forms of reptiles as pets, and the rats to along with them .... snake-food. People's outlook of snakes was how ugly, long and slimy snakes were, and before meeting my friend, I too thought this.

It was only through being exposed to and slithered on, that I was able to receive the knowledge that snakes were not the way that were made out to be.

Rats were also something that I got to terms with, as he also bread rats to feed the snakes, and I ended up with a rat as a pet for nearly six years. The concept to people was and still is beyond their limits, and because of what other people may feel about something, others tend to think that they obviously know better due to exposure, so that is the way it is.

From this I began to take on life with a different outlook. Instead of only believing what I could be proved or see, I began to work backwards - I would take everything on, and then keep an open mind about it.

If I was the man whose friend saw the UFO, my new approach would be, "Well, I have not seen one myself, but tell me what you can about it", then in my mind I would store this UFO information and perhaps someone else would tell of a similar tale, or even I would see one, and then rule it in or out.

To completely close yourself off to possibilities means that you would be missing out on life itself. Once someone proves your idea beyond reasonable doubt, then you can rule it out for now, until maybe another possibility of the same idea comes out.

Before you met, or spoke or saw a picture of your cousin, which you only heard about - did you believe that you had that cousin, just from what your mother told you, although you had no proof?

Life is about choices, try not to fill the spaces with blanks - be open to what this vast universe has to offer, and then decide if it works or not for yourself. What some people swear by, others will curse - so make up your own mind, and allow the boundaries to be flexible according to the time, place, situation and circumstance.

"Don't doubt until you have the full evidence, but be logical when choices need to be made."

Chapter 33

Mistakes Or Lessons

- Did you do that?
- Who is responsible for the mess in here?
- No- that's wrong - do it again!
- Cant you do anything right?
- How many times do I have to tell you how to do it that way?

Does any of this sound familiar to you? I bet that you know when it was said and who said it to you, and for what reason, and exactly the tone in which it was said.

Why all the negativity? Why can't people let us grow and make mistakes, why can't we make the same mistakes that other people made when they were doing it the first time? Why is everyone expected to grasp everything first time, and not ever mess up!

Am I wrong in thinking that life is about growing and developing? Does this not happen by continuing to take in information, process it and then use it where you can and mainly for the same reason you took the information in? Are we not continuing to learn each day something new?

Why can a "normal" person not be able to or allowed to learn slower than the other "normal" person? If he/she has a learning disability, it is accepted that they are more likely to take on information and process it slower than a "normal" person, but who says that normal people are all at the same level of processing?

School classes are made for this very reason, and they try to group people of the same speed together, class A, B, C, D, E, F, G, H, and I, yes I, I was in an I class at one stage at school, where the year had so many people in it.

The classes staggered according to previous years marks, or as I say "Processing capability" at about 28 people per class and I was processing slowly - very slowly.

Anyway, this was one of the most successful years at school, because the 16 of us were not expect to fly through the work, but by having the pressure taken off us in this way.

For the first time there was a real opportunity to understand, listened to as an individual, and this got me "promoted" into the E class the following year.

How many times did Einstein experiment with different things before they worked, and how many times did the Wright brothers and others try and fly before it worked? How many rockets did they try and send to space before they succeeded?

If all this is so acceptable that in order to succeed we ought to try, try and try again until it works, and yet these days, this philosophy seems to have left the homes of many, because people are often complaining about making a mistake and really getting it. It could be from the boss, a parent, teacher or manager or someone who has already completed the work, and can do it without fail, but I wonder how many times that person tried back when they were first learning it?

Why do we "expect" others to foul-up and when they do it's okay, but when we foul-up it is the end of the world! We all seem to be doing things "wrong" in the eyes of: parents, friends, lovers, partner, colleagues, or generally people around you on a daily basis. Are you happy with what they do? Do you complain about them?

When was the last time that you complimented someone, for doing what he or she were doing right or wrong, but were trying? I know that many men take for granted the fact that their wife, lover or partner whom they are with will do their washing, ironing, cooking, cleaning amongst other things too.

To those men or women in this position - when last did you thank that person in your life? I am not meaning, "Thank you for dinner, that was lovely", but a meal out or a box of chocolates or concert or something from you to them to show your appreciate, and that does not mean a new Iron, or Washing Machine so they can do the work better for you. Thank the person after every load of wash or ironing, every meal, every time they cleaned up for you and make it sincere.

These are lesson opportunities, which you can take, and start working with. Start complimenting others, and they will start to look for the good in you and not the "mistakes" which are providing opportunities on which you can continually grow and develop.

"Something tried and something failed, is a lesson well learnt
Failure provides the individual with real life experience from which to
grow and develop - that first-time success never will"

Chapter 34

Choice

- What's it going to be?
- Whose is going to go first?
- When will you leave?
- What shall I make for dinner today?
- How much money should I invest?
- Which way shall I go home?
- Which ice cream shall I take for desert?
- Shall I go shopping or not?
- Will I help my brother with his chores?

The answer to all of this is - that which makes you feel best!

It's yours all yours, and don't let people bully you into believing that it is not, and getting you to do what they want you to do, for them.

Choice - what is it? Choice is choosing, making a decision between things, taking into yourself the option, which is most suitable for your needs with regard to the topic at hand.

So if that is what choice is all about, then why do we have such difficulty with it? Why do we make mountains out of molehills?

If I gave you the following list of items as presented on a menu, tick off the 3 items to quench your pallet

Vegetarian quiche	____	Lasagna	____
Spaghetti	____	Tripe	____
Shepherds Pie	____	Irish stew	____
French Salad	____	Stuffed Garlic Mushrooms	___
Fillet Steak	____	Salmon Steak	____

Are you sure that those are the 3 to satisfy your hunger needs at the next meal if it was offered to you? To be certain check that menu one more time just to make sure.

Congratulations - You have just demonstrated the Power Of Choice, so now you now that you have just proved to yourself that you can do it. Now, because you did this, the rest of the chapter will be easier to understand.

After having been stimulated by different feeling, thoughts and emotions, you came to a decision as to which of the foods presented on the menu would suit your needs best, at this particular moment.

With each name on the menu, comes a memory of one sort or another, it may be of a bad experience with that particular dish, you have a dislike to a dish for a particular reason, and what happens as you are reading or thinking about each name, presented in your brain to you will be the memory of: taste, likeness to it, a body reaction to that stimulus.

If it is something you liked, your body would react in a good positive way, where the taste buds start causing the mouth to water, and the tummy seems to get excited at the thought of the dish, and a warm comforting feeling radiates instantly throughout your body which will be taken as a good approving sign, which you will respond to by acceptance or refusal - the choice is made!

Something else on the menu however, may cause the opposite or a reaction not quite as comforting or "appetizing" and will not cause any sort of wonderful exciting reaction to your body. The body, if you really don't like the item, may actually give a funny taste into the mouth, and give you goose bumps or just the "yuk" feeling throughout.

To take this even further, we are going to do a small process.

First of all, think of something really sad, or distressing for a minute. Try and remember as much about it as possible for just a minute... Now

LIVE LIFE LIKE A BUMBLEBEE

shift your focus from the thought to how your body is responding in feeling of comfort, weight, and easiness.

- Is it light or heavy?
- Do you feel good or bad?
- Would you prefer to get up and dance or go to bed?
- Is the general feeling about you good or bad in the moment of SADNESS?

DO THIS AGAIN BEFORE READING ON TO REALLY FEEL THOSE SENSATIONS.

Okay, part one of this exercise is complete - now shift your mind and body back into the present time as you sit or lie or however you may be as you read this. How is your body feeling now that it is back to normal?

For the next few moments - think of the most powerful, exciting, happy, joyous moment of your life, and allow those emotions to fill your body as you remember and feel that moment or time once again.

- How does your body react to that thought?
- Do you feel light or heavy?
- Does it feel pleasant or unpleasant?
- Are you dancing or going to bed after thinking that?
- Are you feeling trodden all over or feeling untouchable?

So, from our little exercise, we have now twice proved the connection between the mind and the body, as demonstrated by yourself with your own physical response. With positive thoughts on the mind, the body feels great and wonderful, and with negative thoughts, the body feels flat and under- powered, ready to give up and go to bed.

By feeling good, we know that it is likely to be the right thing to choose, and because it leaves such a wonderful after- effect-so why not. The

144

negative is sooooo heavy and burdening; it is no wonder that sick people feel the way they do - so try your best to cheer them up.

I know that you would like to feel better about life, and yourself more often, because I knew that when I was offered the choice by the universe to either feel lousy and sad, or make my life work for me, I chose the way I now prefer to live - for me.

The Power Of Choice works like this. Imagine yourself in the top brick of the pyramid. Even better would be for you to take an A4 sheet of paper and redraw a pyramid like this one. Place yourself in the top brick.

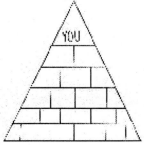

FIG 1 - You in charge of your pyramid.

Fig 1.
This is your Life Choice Pyramid, and it is about your choices that you will be making on a daily, momentary or long-term basis.

Now, before we go on, I would like you to fill in the rest of your Pyramid with the names of those people around you on a daily basis, and who are most likely to interact with you.

This will be people like: parents, family, relatives, work colleagues, social friends and other people with whom you would consider have a place in your life.

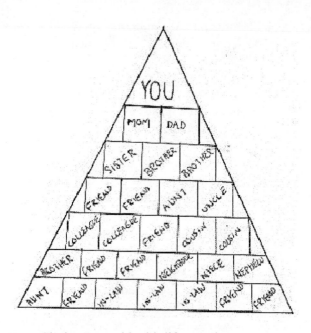

FIG 2 - Your Choice Pyramid with life members.

This is how yours may look once done.

The next thing to do is to think of the most recent question asked of you where someone wanted you to make a choice or decision. Write it in below:

....
....
....…...............
.………………………………………………………………………………
……………..

Read it back to yourself and then write down the answer you gave and the action you took:

....
....

146

....
....

Now ask yourself the following questions:

Who benefited by your actions? Tick the answer/s.
A: YOU ALONE   _____ (You in the top of your
                                                pyramid)

B: YOU AND OTHERS   _____ (Others being the people
                                                affected by the actions)
C: OTHER PEOPLE   _____ (Only other people and not
                                                yourself)
D: NOBODY   _____ (People who are not even in
                                                your pyramid)

If your answer was:
A - then that is great, that kind of response will keep you on top of your Choice Pyramid, and in control of your choices, and so your life.

B - You and Other People, - ask yourself, was it convenient, or did you go out of your way to please the other person? If you did it because YOU wanted to, then that is great, and the other person was lucky enough to be able to share in that with you. Be careful that you don't allow people to manipulate you off the top and out of making your own choices.

C: -& D is both about you doing things for the well-being of other people when you have your own things to be done and to get done, so do not benefit by being manipulated. Unless it is your work and you are being paid for it, then you are really wasting your time.

Your new objective should be to begin stopping this from happening, so that you will not be used for other peoples benefit at your own expense.
In combination to this WHO BENEFITS formula, combine this with how you feel inside and how your body reacts to the thought of doing what

you have been asked to decide on. In my opinion there are two ways to decide, ask yourself: WHO BENEFITS?

As with the menu, see what your body does, and that would give you a good idea of whether to do it or not. The thought of that particular idea becoming a part of your life or not should be enough to decide if you would like to take it on or not.

We all have it within us to know if we want something or not, so that's not the problem. Problems arise out of guilt - guilt of not doing what others expect you to do, which in most cases is for their benefit and not yours, although you are manipulated into believing that it is for your benefit too -"Thanks for the lift - I'll see you at midnight for the lift home!" would be a good example.

This is the reason that people have started to make mountains out of molehills. Instead of being honest to another person by saying we don't want to do something, we make up this big wondrous story to make it more important, and to have an excuse to not do what they would like you to be doing with them.

Having had lots of practice in making excuses for other people, we start to make them for ourselves as to why we should not or cannot do things.

When it comes to Choice, I find that the best way to get the courage to do something that I have not done before, and don't know if I wont like it is say to myself, "It will either do your brain in, or be great", or "It will either work or it won't", and the other one would be "It is either yes or no", and this usually keeps me focused on making choices for my own good.

Think of all the "stress" that people put themselves through trying to decide, or trying to make up a good excuse, when all they need to say is, "No thank you", or "Yes, I would like that", but instead sit on the "maybe, perhaps, I'll think about it or I'm not quite sure yet".

How convinced do you feel when another tells you one of those answers? I am not convinced at all. It is very seldom that someone who tells you that they will think about it actually do go ahead with it. The reason being, is that intuitively you will know if something will work for you, instinct I guess, so why draw it out?

When asked a question, and you are expected to answer by making a choice or decision, it comes almost automatically - because like food on a menu, it will instantaneously appeal to you or it won't. It's only where something is completely new to you, which you may need to think about it but even then, the idea will either grab you or get your interest, or it won't.

I heard a saying once that says, "DON'T KNOCK IT UNTIL YOU HAVE TRIED IT", and this rings true to me. I am not saying that you should go and do all sorts of illegal things because you have not tried it, but be logical, and don't harm yourself or anyone else whilst doing or trying something new.

Life is about continual growth and developments, and when you make a choice, take personal responsibility for that choice and trust that it is what you need to be doing and that you are learning from it.

When another person benefits from your choice, and you don't - it means that you have been knocked off the top of YOUR Choice Pyramid, by allowing another person to make a decision / choice for you ...... tastes like rotten eggs to me - how does that taste in your mouth or make you feel?

"Listen to Your Body - It Knows More Than You Think"

Chapter 35

Goals & Accomplishments

A goal is something that would display a result of work done up until that point, and certain work is going to be the reason for achieving that particular goal. To reach this goal will be something that will reward you with a sense of contentment and fulfillment. It is something that you want to do for yourself in most cases, although others may also benefit from you accomplishing it.

Goals should be both short and long term ideas, which focus in the same direction, as pertaining to your ideals, for present and future. A goal is a stepping-stone in the right direction, and once achieved it is a landmark, which reflects how far you individually have come from where you first started. From this point set your next goal. As individuals we all have our own personal levels, which would mark success or achievement.

Don't worry about the number of stepping-stones that there may be on your path, but focus on the one in front of you. When you get to that one then the next, just make sure that they are going in the right direction for you, and soon enough you will be there.

Sure enough, there are always ups and downs - but that's life, and without them we would not strengthen through each challenge presented to us.

Think for a minute about the times when there were no cars, and everything was by foot or by mule or horse, or wagon. These people, to even think of traveling from home to town or on a journey had a form of pilgrimage, rather than a trip. In those times, a trip to town may have taken a day or even a few days to get there and back. They may have had to sleep along the road, or take along some form of "canvas" under which to rest and shelter.

Also to consider back then were the challenges of nature, where you were just as much of a target to a wild animal as a sheep or deer may have been... and without much for protection.

Not only were the wild animals perhaps seeing you as prey, but the bandits also knew that most traveling were coming or going from a town, which meant a chance of money or food and purchases to be acquired, created a worthwhile target out of any traveler.

A trip like this would have taken some planning, both short term and long term, where goals were set and to achieve them would have meant to get into town safely and unharmed, make the trade necessary, and then complete the goal by getting safely home.

In term of goals: the long term goals would have been the getting to town and the getting home again, while the short term goals would have been: safe travel, food, shelter, staying alive overnight, and each village would have been considered a short term goal.

It is the elements, trials and challenges of nature and other men that would have stood between man reaching and fulfilling his objective.

Although so much has changed, so little has changed. Without realizing it we are continually setting goals even in today's modern world.

Be it on a day where you will be going to the Big City, and coming home in the evening, consists of: leaving one point and hope to- your goal is to reach the next particular town 100kms away, then that is the main goal.

The short term goals would be things like not having an accident, not running out of fuel which means stopping at the relevant places, and keeping yourself focused so as not to miss the turn off and other traveling conditions which need to be considered. And lets not forget the bandits - they are still there, but now more rough, violent and have they guns.

Another example would be the chores within a family on a day-to-day basis, which range from being both big and small, however unless all of them are done - very little progress will be made in that household.

Life has become almost automatic for many of us, and especially the people that do the same work everyday, like a mother: -

- She gets up earlier than the rest of the family to prepare meals for the family,
- Gets the family out of bed,
- Gets them organized for the day
- Sends them or takes them to where they need so be - college, school, play or work.

People, who are not mothers, may not realize that the mother's day does not end there but begins only once all are out from under her feet. She will have a goal for the end of the day - likely to have finished: the cooking, cleaning and other daily household chores, by the time the family is home, or has to be collected.

For this goal, she must set herself stepping-stones in the right direction, which will mark and show her the level of achievement throughout the day.

Having already begun early in the morning, to prepare breakfast and the schoolwork and college meals, she then has to get the family up, fed and out on time. This will be her first goal for the day.

Once the family is out of the house:
- It is clearing up the breakfast dishes
- Cleaning the house
- Cleaning up after other people who should clear up after themselves
- Put on some washing
- Do the ironing

- Plan dinner
- Make sure of the times that the kids are all finishing, or if they will be picked up later
- Go grocery shopping
- On the way to fetch the kids
- Feed the pets on returning from shopping
- Get kids out of school clothes and out from under the feet and off the clean carpet
- Fetch other kid from sports practice
- Finish cooking dinner
- Partner arrives home - serve dinner
- Clean up
- Help kids with homework
- Ensure kids are bathed and ready finished homework before television
- Ready for bed by a reasonable hour which may very well include dragging them away from the Nintendo or Television
- Partner needs a rub-down from a long tiring day at work and the business lunch went on for hours
- Check that the animals are where they should be or secure for the night
- She finally bathes herself, and then collapses into bed... with a snoring partner who keeps her from decent nights' sleep, even though she is exhausted.

That is about a normal day – what about the added challenges when there is also:
- Sick people
- Sick animals
- Parent teacher visits
- Mother-in-law unexpectedly visits
- Neighbors come by to catch up on gossip
- Partner hints at wanting to spend some time together
- Kids are feeling left out – make special time for each of them

… And then somehow find time for her.

The importance of setting goals is quite clear to a person in this situation, who has to ensure that certain things are done by certain times, and that becomes her stepping stone, and then the next few things that have to be completed by a specific time, would be the next stepping stone, and so on throughout the day.

Setting more direct goals would help this kind of person out of unnecessary situations by having a goal like:

- Kids would help prepare the meals
- Kids would do things like the dishes as well as clear up after themselves.

Once this was taught to the kids, it would give her more time for herself, the kids themselves and then later on more time for her partner. Pass on the responsibility to the kids to feed and groom their pets, ensure that where the family is capable of doing a share of the work -its done that way.

The family don't see the hard work that needs to be done while nobody is about, so they won't think about things like this - it is up to the mother to set these goals that will best suite her needs, and limited time.

It is now time that you set your own goals, as an individual - not a family member. Perhaps start with a list of "things" that you want to do, achieve, have, obtain or even display, so you personally know that you are working towards the things that you want for you.

"Make each day count by keeping it focused on your goals"

Chapter 36

Your Gift To The World

It comes at some stage in everyone's life - the question of, "What is my gift to the world, what is my purpose? - What am I supposed to do, to contribute?"

The answer to that is YOU and your gift to the world is YOU being YOU!

Think of life as we know it - cars, planes, trains, technology, space - travel, deep sea works... etc., etc. ... now, go back to the caveman: - wearing skins, being hunted, hunting, stone utensils, living like an animal.

Over time, from either two thousand or a thousand more years ago, "man" as human being has continued to develop and grow within, and has carried this over into his surroundings, which have somewhat changed from a cave, to a high-rise penthouse or months in space at a time.

With primitive knowledge, he learned about fire, with which he could warm himself as well as cook. He learned to make tools, warming-wraps from the skins, and then over time finer clothes and finer elements through weaving and sewing.

He developed the wheel, on which he could carry a load and transport more than he alone could normally carry. He learned to domesticate wild animals into animals from which he could stock and harvest his food in one location instead of having to live chasing them.

He learned to create light, at night, power, energy all over time, and the development began, so he made life easier for himself. The development took place from perhaps one mans idea with the wheel, or it may have been a sharp rock to be used to cut and dig, the idea seen and demonstrated to another who may have added something like a handle or a different tool from the first idea. The ideas were allowed to grow and develop from one individual to the next each adding their own little bit, and now look in your shed at the digging tools we now use.

By sharing your knowledge and ideas, allows others to add their own ideas to yours, to make something new or to improve your concept, for which you are likely to have been inspired by someone else's idea.

Go back again to the first people - they had nothing other than that which nature provided: water heat, pressure, natural rock, stone's, minerals, animals and the elements that make up the most basic of outdoor living.

From the ideas started off by those people way back in their caves, we a few thousand years later are living in space, high rise buildings, and in an "evolved" place, which is still continuing to grow and develop.

So what is it that you can offer? What is your gift to the world?

Your gift is everything that you do. Everything that you do is based upon information thoughts and ideas which have grown and developed over many years from the first man to all those before you, until now - you yourself. It is on this education that those thoughts and ideas will be shared with others who can themselves add to it to help the growth and development of the idea to a further level.

From sand, stone, minerals, water, heat, pressure, vegetation, animals, seasons, cycles and the elements that make up the most basic form of nature - man has taken those elements and converted them into:

Space travel, supersonic travel, air travel, cars, planes, trains, machines, weapons, artificial organs, cloning animals, lasers, surgery, electricity, buildings - but remember that all these concepts have come from what nature had to offer then, and what it has to offer now – which all began with pretty much what is out in your garden!

A space shuttle is made from nature - sand makes the glass, stones and minerals are responsible for the metals, plants give paper, glue, rubber, animals provide the models and basic structure design, elements of wind, water and fire, pressure and heat are used to put it all together and to help it fly, minerals to make the runways, by-products of the mineral oil to create fuel, and other elements combined which come from nature directly or indirectly, to create the computers and the most elaborate of technical and electronic equipment.

We really have come far, merely from sharing ideas with one another, so share your gift to the world by sharing your idea with others, and take your place in making it what it is today, and will become tomorrow.

*"Everything you do, has an effect on something or someone else,
so be aware of what you are doing"*

Chapter 37

Last Words

Many people will try to help another by saying a variety of things, in trying to help others where they can .... Are they in fact helping? In some cases I would say "Yes", and in most cases I would say "No". Let me explain the concept of growth and development then you can decide for yourself.

Start with a butterfly in its cocoon. Watch and see how long the butterfly takes to come out of that cocoon. It might be hours, minutes or even a day or two. Once it comes out, it stretches its wings, and allows them to dry before lifting off to begin its life in flight.

Have you ever wondered why this is possible? - Most animals need time "learn to walk" or "practice flying" before getting going - not straight away. So maybe a Butterfly does not fly in a straight line which means we cannot tell if it is making a good job of flying or not, but it flies first time.

Nature has provided us all with the strength to do what we need to do within our own environment. Life, at many stages seems an awful struggle, but nature has its reasons.

As with the butterfly, some changes take longer to complete than others, but that all depends on the individual.

Consider the butterfly - it did not give up, it rested a bit at times, sometimes for short periods and sometimes for longer periods, and once feeling strong again, continued to work it 's way out of the cocoon.

Compare yourself to the butterfly. Sometimes you might feel that life is that struggle, and no matter how hard you work to move, you just feel stuck. But, as with the butterfly being stuck and struggling to work

ITSELF through, the struggle is actually making you stronger by enduring the period of difficulty and being able to come out stronger on the other side.

Many people in a situation where things seem hopeless think that this is a useless time in their life and not worth the trouble of living it, when in actual fact it is a very valuable time. Without it, it becomes difficult to move forward through life whether you are a butterfly or a human.

If you were to help a butterfly out of the cocoon, by breaking open the cocoon, the butterfly would come out – who in their right mind would turn away from an open door knowing that this is going to make life that much easier, and that your other option is a period of struggle?

It ill then allows its wings to dry and then will drop off and die within a few hours. The reason being is that it needs first of all to eat the cocoon to get some "fuel", and then the "struggle" of getting out ensures that it becomes strong enough to fly and face the world once it finally does get out.

You too need to struggle through metamorphosis (changing periods of your life), but are not to see it as a time of being stuck, rather a time of learning and strengthening to prepare for what is to come.

Believe that nature will place these strengthening tasks ahead of you so that in overcoming them you are stronger for challenges ahead.

In nature all sorts of creatures are strengthened and educated through challenge and hardship. This not only educates, but also exposes and prepares the animal as to what may lie ahead, for survival. In nature only the strong survive, to ensure that only a good line of breed remains to repopulate the next generation, and here the predators would ensure that the "weak" don't go to waste.

So now with your new outlook on the "hard times", you can see the "weakening" that other people are offering you, although it may seem that they are trying to help.

A Counselor is a good example of what we are talking about here – they will always allow you to make the choices, through reflecting back to you your own situation from a different perspective. This allows you to see the bigger picture – as soon as people TELL you what to do; they are helping you out of your cocoon, which is ultimately weakening you through a lack of life experience.

Help is really about offering a lifeline of support to encourage the individual with what they are doing, and edge along in your own direction. When you are fearful of doing that which you would really like to do – it means that it is an opportunity to experience, and grow. Let others support and offer guidance, but make sure that you strengthen your own wings, because by other people strengthening their wings will not make you fly any easier.

So now in leaving you, I leave you with the following words of "experience"!

**"Don't walk the well-trodden path of others before you,
But walk creating your own path where others may follow"**

Best Of Luck and keep moving forward

Anthony.

Printed in the United Kingdom
by Lightning Source UK Ltd.
2634